Conjecture and Speculation

Common Sense: Not as Prevalent Today as was Thought Yesterday

Clifton Ray Wise Ed.D.

Author: Clifton Ray Wise Ed.D.

Digital Epub : 979-8-9917742-5-3

Paperback : 979-8-9917742-6-0

Publisher: Clifton Ray Wise

A C K N O W L E D G E M E N T S

I want to thank all those human entities who have lapse in judgement. You know, the human entities that never sit down and add the pros and cons of topics before they make a stance, open their mouth and ramble, or mistakenly join a cause.

This writing is for you. You gave me the topics of discussion. Without your assistance this writing would not have been possible. Some human entities have the sense god gave a horse and some do not. I can only guess that is why the term "horse sense" traveled from the sparsely populated prairies to the densely populated cities.

PROLOGUE

The premise of this writing is simple. I don't know if I am like other human entities, or if I am one of a kind? Each day I see or hear about things that make little to no sense or no sense at all to me. Maybe I think a little too deeply sometimes, about certain topics? Maybe I expect more from human elements than I typically get? This is a culmination of some such topics. This isn't really an opinion piece this is more questioning than anything else. Well, I am sure opinions will abound. Maybe I am the one missing something? Maybe not? I like to make people think. I like to make students think. I am not looking for followers that want to jump on my wagon. My wagon probably has a few broken wheels anyway.

Discussing topics these days is like talking to Archie Bunker. He knew what he knew and that was it. It was difficult to get him to sway his opinion. Even with a topic you thought you could surely win; he still defied all logic and common sense. Common sense, now that is a stretch word. Sense isn't so common nor is it prevalent. That is the reason for this writing. Common sense is something we take for granted and so is plain old horse-sense.

INTRODUCTION

Why do we bother to think in the first place? We use high sounding terms like creative and critical thinking. When we think of a lot of the things in life that cause us to ponder can we actually say that someone puts much thought into those in the first place? Really? Or did they just throw something out there in the spur of the moment? They just filled a gap within an instant. They needed an answer fast and that is what they did. They came up with one and the population never questioned it. Never gave it a second thought. Here we are.

Comedians pop into my head when I think about some of the things I have seen and heard throughout my years that make no sense. Gallagher and George Carlin make a lot of sense calling attention to things like these. I am not going to steal their fire or thunder, as I have encountered a lot of things throughout my 60 years that stand out as, well, "whose bright idea was that"?

Table of Contents

Where Are Things?

This was to be my last topic in the writing, but at the end I decided it should be my first as there is a lot of speculation and conjecture here, even my own. I had to put it someplace or to at least give it honorable mention. There are things from our human history that have been hidden, misplaced, etc.

One of those things is the Ark of the Covenant. If you believe in the book, we have all heard of? Where is it? Is it in a vast military warehouse of artifacts? That was in a movie once. It is in the tunnels under the Vatican. Who saw it last? Just curious. Am I the only human entity that thinks about these things?

If we know about some of human history, Adolph Hitler had his minions searching, stealing, and documenting religious artifacts from anywhere they could find and get their hands on them. Then I would say many of them were the reason behind the Catholic church helping Nazi war criminals escape from being captured at the end of WWII. If you research a little on the internet some of these artifacts, come out from time to time in the press and who was it that had possession of these historical artifacts. Ancestors of those war criminals. Although, I do not see all Germans as war criminals, just the ones who followed the inhumane leadership. I guess some could say they were just following orders. That is another discussion, not for this topic. These artifacts had been handed down over the years and were accidentally found.

Where is the Holy Grail? No, it isn't in the Monty Python movie of the same name. It wasn't in Life of Brian either. Someone is keeping them a secret. Was it the Star of India that got misplaced in the Pink Panther movie? Is it still missing? I think you see where I get my humor from. I grew up watching the first years of Saturday Night Live. "Knock, Knock, Knock…Who is it? Landshark".

This stuff has to be somewhere, where is it, or where are they? Can we take a peek into the catacombs of the Vatican?

And what about those Aliens from outer space that tripped to the good ole USA in the fifties and sixties? Where are they? Where did they go? Were they put somewhere? One of my favorite questions is on this whole planet called earth, why did they choose the USA as a destination point? Were they just tired of traveling and just make a pit stop and got held hostage? What is the deal? Were we the good ole boys at the bar and saw the newcomers and said "hey, come on up to the bar gents and have a beer" then we knocked them on the head and well, you know the outcome. Supposedly. Is everything, supposedly?

C o m m o n   S e n s e

I was speaking with my buddy the other day on the phone, and we were discussing the human population. We were laughing about the term common sense and how truly uncommon it was. We said it should be named uncommon sense as that was a better delineation as it seemed like very few human entities were in tune with this acquired trait. We thought that this was a more common trait with the addition of time, although time really did not make it certain that you would grasp the concept of sense.

Is God Really to Blame

Everyone wants to put the blame on someone or something other than themselves. I guess they just don't want people to see them in a bad light. Maybe they just have an issue apologizing?

It appears everyone thinks they are a religious entity. They heard a scripture in a sermon once and got the idea they are privy to know something that nobody else knows. It seems as everyone likes to say, "I have read the Bible". They all like to say it, but in actuality have they or is that just an allegation? "I guess they cannot say they allegedly read the Bible. That might lead to a whole other interpretation.

I will not say that I have read the whole Bible, that would be a lie. Do I know a little something that is written within its pages? Yes, I do. Well, I think I have a somewhat correct interpretation. Maybe that is how I should put it.

Is God to blame for all the bad and the good in the world? Well, if you know a little about what is written inside the pages you would say: At this present time, the answer is no! Well, how do you come up with that mister man? Well, I read somewhere that God is not in control of the current situation within the planet, that the entity in control is Satan the devil. Hmmm. That might make some sense. Isn't there something in there about a 1000-year reign and an abyss? I think I read that somewhere. If I was a biblical scholar, I might know that page and or paragraph, but I don't claim to be that learned of biblical facts. I just remember reading that somewhere. I don't think it was in a popular mechanics magazine either.

Somewhere else I read that God was Love or is Love. Maybe that is wrong. It might have said there was a God of Love. Anyway, when you look at all the imperfection within and upon the earth if there was a God of Love and that God of Love was in control then why is there imperfection in the first place? Where did imperfection come from? We were told, or within the pages of this text called the Bible that imperfection is a resultant factor of the Adam and Eve eating the apple blunder. In there it talks about a snake tempting Eve, and that snake is the embodiment of Satan the devil. So, I would infer that the imperfection of mankind was projected forth by this Satan the devil entity rather than this God of Love entity. I am assuming this, but I think I am coming up with this relatively simple finger pointing solution. "The devil made me do it". We have heard that how many times in our lives and maybe used it once or twice. I never heard anyone say, "God made me do it". I think my assumption is reliable, valid, and reasonable. I could be wrong as I was wrong once before.

If God is Love and he/she is in control, then why are there crippled and handicapped children. Why are there homeless populations? Why are there wars? I could go on with a list that would be never-ending. I think we know why, as that entity we speak of is not in control. The blame must lie elsewhere. If you attach the blame elsewhere you can also add the terms of time and circumstance. The stars and planets just aligned in a certain way and that is why things just turned out the way they did. The imperfections of mankind making

5

their way to the surface. Never letting the population forget the cause and the effects. The cause and effects that remind us to not fall privy of the same things again.

I saw a video a while back where a girl was laying with her dog that she was about to have put to sleep. The title was "The devil couldn't reach me, so he took my dog". That was an awakening moment for me. I really thought about that when I saw it. I have had to do the same thing, and it still brings tears to my eyes to this day. That is some enlightenment right there. How prolific and mind changing for me.

I never had realized I had been thinking wrong all these years. I never once blamed God for anything, and I never remember praying for anything either. I never really needed to pray for anything in the past as I always knew I should work for what I wanted, and I would somehow be rewarded. And I always knew life was just the luck of the draw and sometimes things would turn out for the good and sometimes the bad, that was just time and circumstance.

But I always wondered and asked if God was Love why would/should/could he/she let bad things happen to good people? I never got an answer. No preachers could ever give you that answer. From them you get the same blah, blah, blah. With no direct answer. Come to find out, I have known the answer all along I just needed something to smack me in the face and wake me up. I guess I have been slumbering all these years and now I have awakened and have the answer. Do you want to know that answer? God is NOT in control! Satan the devil is in control!

If God was in control, there would be no list of issues for resolve. There would be no questioning. It seems easy to see when it is pointed out and there is a reasonable explanation. Everyone gets so caught up in searching out a belief that they can't see what is in front of their face. What is it they say, "You cannot see the forest for the trees or maybe it's the trees for the forest"?

Moral of the story: "Put the blame where the blame goes".

Church and State

Convocation is a term associated with the church in the earliest history. At that time the church was the main source of education. Now we have similar terms: convocation and graduation. These are like terms but different.

Throughout the United States there is a phrase that goes back many years: The separation of Church and State. Actually, it points out there should be a split between religion and politics. This is where convocations become somewhat confusing. My question would be: If we truly have a separation of church and state then why do public universities feel they have a right to push a religious agenda upon attendees at a function.

If you go to a convocation at a public University, they always have some big church preacher dressed in his shark skin suit and wearing his gators to give a big, long prayer for the university. The administration does not care about the number of attendees that are not of that faith and are not happy with that circumstance when they have no control of optional attendance as it is a mandatory engagement. Is this a violation of church and state? I am not a scholar of that topic either. It does seem a little ridiculous when you call out and pray to an entity that is not in control. In the prayer speech the orator calls out that all the people gathered were brought together by God and that there was or is some prolific reason they all have been gathered. It really does seem a bit showy to me. I guess the average-dressing small church preacher with the 20 parishioners just wasn't a good choice to pray for the big circus event?

Of course, you have those followers in the background that say "Amen" every sentence I guess they seem to agree with. "Amen brother and raise their hands in allegiance".

Then, typically after the long-winded prepared prayer speech there is the Pledge of Allegiance. Now I don't have a problem with this, I just have a question here.

If you have a religious prayer and a political patriotic Pledge, one after the other, somewhat attached, is this not a violation of church and state? It just seems a little questionable to me. I'm just saying. I guess sports assemblies are privy to the same attachment.

Don't get me wrong. I have strong opinions when discussing the downward spiral of discipline in the public educational classrooms. What do you expect to happen when you remove the ideals this United States of America was founded on: Freedom of patriotism and religion. Isn't that what was once called "The American Way?" I think we see what happened when the pledge of allegiance and religion was removed from our US school systems. Yes, it was a form of control, but do we not need some control sometimes? Just curious.

Something Called AI

The new crutch for the incompetent and lazy. The idea of artificial intelligence has been around since when. Do some research if you are not too lazy? I know the answer, you can find it easily. There are reasons why it has not been deeply exposed until now. The human element isn't ready for it. Is the human element ready to have themselves replaced in the workforce? Don't we have a high enough unemployment rate now? And you think it will get better.

We add another human replacing tool to the gambit of others we have developed in the past. Some say "Tomato" and some say "Tomato". I asked Google if Google was an AI tool. Some of the top answers were NO and some were YES. Google came back with NO, and many others came back with YES. Imagine that? The Kettle calling the pot black.

Google gave me a load of crap that AI is a tool, a tool in which Google just happens to have its own version of AI called "Google AI". I guess a lot of thought went into the preparation to answer that question in a non-monopoly sort of way. How many years have search engines been around? Since the 1980s and 90s. Aren't those in reality, AI in the first place? Back then and now you can ask a question and get a myriad of written responses. Now you ask AI, and it gives you a completed version with only a single compiled answer.

There are a few positive things that can come from it that I see, but the many negatives far outweigh those few. The positives would be for the lazy and the unlearned population. Isn't that the general population that suffers the most from unemployment statistics? I guess that is why these newly advanced technologies are not privy or generally easily made accessible to these populations. Because, who cares about their input, right? They won't or don't use those technologies anyway. Making the less educated population even less educated.

What are the negatives you ask? Any technology that replaces human elements, do we really need it? Don't we have enough unemployment as it is? How about a few examples?

The student who has an assignment and uses AI, then turns the work in as his/her own work. Don't laugh, this is the aftermath of AI that is plaguing the educational system to no end! When you project the administration of your educational facility admits and registers into degree programs a student population that has no business in an educational setting in the first place, do you expect the majority of those students to be honest in their assignment submissions. If so, you are sadly mistaken and need another career path for yourself. Just ask your local faculty member. Not an administrator, a faculty member. The faculty member is the only entity that is on the front line with those students that must deal with this artificial intelligence cheating and plagiarism tools.

Then you have the educated masses that use AI to write their e-mails and documentation. This educated mass that has become stagnant in their learning, and or lazy, and or wanting you to think they are something they are not. Last year I was the Chair of a committee reviewing policies. There were thirty in total. As a team we received the batch of policies for review. We ran all the policies through a plagiarism checker and found all of them to be 100% copied and pasted. We had a good laugh about that one. We had always been told the person in charge of putting these together was an exceptional administrator and scholar. Well, that just proved one thing. That human entity was nothing more than a facade. Of course, we had that idea in the first place as this entity had stolen work from others in the past and called that work his own.

In another example I see long drawn-out and extremely lengthy e-mails that are 100% AI generated from peers. By using these tools are you trying to make yourself believe how smart you think you are or are you trying to make others believe you are that smart? It gets rather comical sometimes. I guess if you receive one of these AI generated e-mails you can go to AI and generate an answer and send it back, courtesy of AI.

It is very easy to see where the incompetence lies within a facility. The entity that yesterday knew nothing of a topic and today they use big words and express that they are the all-knowing. They are the today all-knowing and the yesterday illiterate. When these entities start talking the flashing sign above their head goes off and it also becomes quite comical. You know them, the ones that you have reviewed their educational background, and it has nothing to do with the topic at hand. But they profess they know all and these are the decision makers. You know, the decision makers that always have an extensive answer to every question. The ones that question every question. The ones that make the decisions and do not ask any of the subject matter experts, faculty or lower-level staff. We all know the ones the shiny suits with all the flash and no substance.

Yesterday you could not even spell the topic, and today you are the all-knowing. What a schmuck. You are lying, stealing, and cheating just like the students you chastise for doing the same. I guess that is why they promote the use of artificial intelligence as this has made them what they seem to be today. The best way to hide is to be right out in the open for all to see. It is sad when you see that someone is so insecure and that they need to hide from their own reality. I guess the real sad part this that everyone around them sees the falsehoods that surround them. It would be sad to have no real substance, honor or integrity. Just sad.

I find it rather comical that on one side of the coin AI is being pushed down the throats of everyone on the planet to use it and on the other hand everyone on the plant is complaining about it and likening it to cheating and saying that if you use AI you must sign a disclaimer stating that you used it. Remember when your parents told you to do something and they seemed to have done the opposite? Remember what they said when you asked about it? "Do as I say not as I do". Sounds rather familiar to me. My question would be: Does the usefulness out-weight the consequence?

Black and or African

Well, can you be a combination? Well, I could guess you can, but you can also be White and African. Bear with me as this might be for you. (Is it Bare or Bear? I never really knew or got a correct answer.). Let us get one misconception right out into the sunlight. Just because you are dark-skinned does not mean you are from Africa. It appears many dark-skinned human elements in the United States have the assumption, they have roots in Africa. I cannot truly say all of them, as I have been learned from some of those human entities through what they have told me.

I have had some student parents tell me they have no association with Africa, and they are Black Americans. Then I have others who have told me they have roots in Africa, and they are African Americans. Then I have others that have combined the two and say they are to be denoted as being Black African Americans. Wow, that seems to be a lot to grasp and a wide array of labels. If you know anything about the human element, we have a lot of labels. Labels upon labels upon labels. Some positive and some negative.

How about we start with a base? Maybe our US government knows something we don't? Don't laugh. I know that seems funny. I can laugh the most as I am the one writing this conjecture. Whenever you go to a site or fill out a document there is no such delineation as Black African or African American that I have ever seen, unless I have missed something. There is something the world population needs to know: There are White Africans and there are Black Africans. Black is not the only color in Africa, contrary to popular knowledge. One of my questions would be: If there is a scholarship for Africans or African Americans are they open to White one's a as well as Black one's? Maybe that is why there currently exists no such delineation within US documentation.

Since we never have actually found the ark of Noah. So, we have no idea where it landed after the water deluge, if you are a believer. Wherever the ark would have or may have landed would be from where all inhabitants of this planet came from. I don't think the impression has ever been that we are all of African descent as the ark may have landed upon that continent. There is some speculation that the arc was to have landed somewhere upon the continent of Asia. So, would this make all inhabitants upon the earth today of Asian descent? The discussion here is of a dark-skinned population. I guess the speculation is still up for grabs if proof rears its head. Do other countries or continents have dark-skinned populations? What about the Aborigines of Australia? Do some of them not wear dark skin? They are not from Africa, that I know of.

D E I P i e

DEI seems to be a whole pie. I call it the DEI pie. It seems you either want the whole pie or none of the pie. Is it really one big pie that revolves around three pieces that must be eaten together? Can you have D without the E and without the I? Can you have D and E without the I? How about any other combination? There are three terms that are consistently used together as a whole. Are the three of them basically drawn-out words that mean the same thing? Like some say "Tomato" and some say "Tomato"? I have never seen any of them used separately. I guess it is DEI or nothing. They ALL three must be used in conjunction with each other. "We want it all or nothing". I guess it is just one of those curiosity things. I think some of those terms may be large enough to stand on their own. Does the human element succumb to one of the faults? Greed? Or can we start with one piece then enjoy if we get asked to be given another?

D i v e r s i t y

I was going to make this diversity and inclusion then decided they were not really the same thing. What is diversity? Would I be safe in assuming that diversity means to introduce and add something foreign and make it the norm? That might be difficult to grasp, how about this. If there exists a public University that admits and enrolls a predominant race or creed population of students, then being diverse would mean that the University will pursue admission and enrollment of any other race or creed other than their dominant current race or creed. It must be a public University as a private one does not receive the federal or state funding and does not have to participate honestly in the realm of education. In layman terms: A Predominant White Institution (PWI) to seek diversity would look to enroll any other student race, creed, or color than White. Right? It makes sense to me.

Why is it that they do not do this? They do not do this, and they still call it diversity or being diverse. Seems like smoke and mirrors. Does anyone ever check out the statistics or does anyone really care? They say they are diverse! Are they really? Speaking of smoke and mirrors they often bypass the diverse loophole and search for international students of the same race, color, or creed that dominate their campus in the first place, not really attaining a true goal of true diversity. And as a fact they get away with it. True discrimination at its finest!

I charge some Universities with following this pattern of underhandedness. To be truly honest and truly diverse you must seek out and admit the opposite student population that you currently have. Do some research on those student populations to see if they have diversity initiatives that are being supported by the government and see what their true student population is. This is public information and should be available to everyone if it is a public institution. A lot of money siphons through our educational systems, only to be used not for the purposes it was delineated or intended. Do you really care, or do you just say you do?

E q u a l i t y

Is equality one of those things that "we all get a trophy just for showing up"? Does that mean we are all equal? Some of us are better at baseball than others. Some of us are better writers than others. Some of us are better talkers than others. What does equality mean? Does it mean we all should have a chance at the same successes that others may find? Should we all have the same opportunities? Of course, we should, except, we must look at each human entity separately. We have always heard terms like affirmative action and nepotism. Does affirmative action or nepotism bring equality? Even on the surface neither are a means of bringing forth equality by any stretch.

Affirmative action was touted as bringing one race closer to receiving opportunities than another race was receiving. Kind of a stepping-stone equality program. How many years did it exist, and did it work? It started in the 1960's and ended around 2023. Affirmative action was employment non-discrimination. From what I hear and have heard from others, it never helped anyone or anything. For every single person that said it worked for them you will find another person who says it did not. It just added more complications. Did you ever hear of the bright idea "No child left behind"? Well, that was another brainchild that just didn't pan out.

I don't claim to be equal to anyone. I don't think anyone can claim to be equal to me. We are all different. From the day we are born the five senses of our human bodies gather data, good and bad, and that accumulation of data makes each of us who we are, whether we stand out from the crowd of hide behind the crowd. I don't want everyone to be just like me. I doubt that everyone wants to be just like me. We are all different and we each stand out or sink back.

What about nepotism? Well, that will never be halted. The world is still a place where human entities give other human entities a helping hand. Some of those helping hands may be well-deserved and I would guess there are quite a few that are not. You will never stop this; it will just become quieter. Isn't that what friends are for? Friends are there to help you if you need help. What is the harm if you hold those credentials and can complete the task or tasks? It is when you bypass those credentials where the problems may arise.

We are all human entities, and I guess that is where equality ends. We are all equal in the eyes of the lord. Is that a quote? We all have equal rights to live, pay taxes and die.

What are the terms we've all heard: fascism, communism, what else? Look at the countries that have tried those. Do they look like they work? The commercials you see on television where organizations are begging for your dollars. These are the countries that have tried those. Do the people in those commercials look like those terms work? It is a human tragedy.

Do I need to say that if everyone was equal everyone would limit what they do? You can work 10, 20, 30, 40, 50, or 60 hours a week and everyone is the same. How long do you think everyone will continue to work those hours? Who would work 40, 50, or 60 hours if you got the same pay as 10, 20, or 30? Do many humans really work for the goodness of the population as a whole? It would look good on paper as all these proposed ventures always do, but there is reality we must deal with when we deal with the human element. Greed is one of the human traits. Greed does not have to be BIG it can be small. We always have "what will I get out of it?" Big greed or small greed, would it really make a difference if we justified and minimized the size of the greed? Is there even a slight difference? I guess the difference is the payoff.

Inclusion

What is inclusion? Inclusion has a similarity to diversity. Sometimes, they are used in the same sentence. Inclusion to me means adding something or including something. Including something that you normally do not include. If you are a hiker and you make friends with a wounded veteran. This wounded veteran is missing one or both of his legs. You ask this veteran to spend the day with you on a hike. You know it will be a task, for both of you, but you feel joy or a certain camaraderie with him/her, and you are willing to do the extra work to have him/her along. This is inclusion to me.

I was flipping through the television channels the other day and for some reason I ended up watching rugby. Don't ask me why. A bunch of sweaty dudes kicking, clawing, shoving, running, for hours and at the end of the match surely, bruised and in pain. Not my idea of a relaxing weekend afternoon. I guess the later part of the day, a pint in each hand at the local pub, is more my speed. Maybe without the pain?

I was just curious; there were no black dudes on either team. They were all white or races other than black. Is there an African team somewhere? Are they black or white Africans? I was just curious. Maybe black dudes don't like rugby? Or is it that rugby doesn't like black dudes. What about inclusion?

A l l   o f   N o n e

Why does it have to be all of none? Do they all intertwine?

R e v e r s e   R a c i s m

What does this really mean? Contrary to the popular belief that is incorrect. If you are reversing racism, then you are stomping it out. If you are driving down the road in your car and you stop and put the gear into reverse, which way are you going? You are not travelling the same path as before you are going in the opposite direction. If racism is the straightforward path, then what is the reverse path of racism? Is there such a word as non-racism? Non-racism is the true reverse of racism. This means to abolish all racism. I don't think that was too hard to resolve, but it seems to be rather difficult to grasp.

I want to know the name of the lame duck who coined the two-word term "reverse racism" and put it into a whole different context and way of thinking. Do human elements just jump on board with every term they hear or see and do not question the validity or reliability of it? Well, in fact, yes, they do, the majority most certainly do. The followers in fact. Followers come up with bright ideas, then they attract followers and become the leaders, then they have a myriad of followers, who in fact have no true concept of what they follow in the first place. I guess this is just the ignorance of the human element.

I have often been told or privy to discussions where the human elements discuss racism as solely the White on Black racism of the Martin Luther King era. Then they espouse "reverse racism" as Black on White. Then they want to stick to this with their dying breath. I guess they got caught up with the term in the beginning and didn't bother to research it further. You know, those followers I spoke of. The followers who are the self-proclaimed leaders leading the charge of ignorance.

I was speaking with a friend the other day and we were talking about the human entity and common sense. He said there was no such thing as common sense! If there were this thing called common sense, then it would be more common and prevalent than it is in the

world today. That was deep and true and how prolific.
I would agree with that assumption.

The   True   End

We are taught throughout our lives that the Civil War
was fought to end slavery for the Black population. It
started as early as I can remember from the history
classes I had when I was a little kid. Was there more to
the Civil War than that? I don't know I wasn't there?
Can you believe everything you read? I had a college
professor during my time of my BS degree, and he
seemed to hold the position that there was more to the
Civil War than just then end of slavery. Was he right?
That opened me to more questions and research. Here
we go again. Too much time on my hands for thinking
too much, but anyway, here goes.

Several questions always came to mind:

1. Was the end of the Civil War the end of slavery?
2. If the Civil War ended slavery, why were there
   any such issues involving rioting and Martin
   Luther King 100 years later?
3. Maybe there was an end to slavery, but this
   didn't really mean this end also brought forth
   equality?
4. Maybe I was just getting confused in
   terminologies and true meanings?

Those questions always seemed to creep up on me
when I thought about things.

The United States President at that time was Abraham
Lincoln. He was against slavery. He wanted to end

slavery in the United States. I am sure there may have been others at that time that may have wanted to end slavery too. I am not delineating a full expose on history here this is pure thinking on my part to try and tie some things together that make sense in my mind.

Every history scholar knows that during the new eastern coast of the US colonization there were ships bringing people to the "New World". During that colonization there was a need for labor and assistance to "break the ground of this new world". The King of England was given the idea of selling prisoners and whomever to this new colonization, that was predominantly backed by England. I think we all know the story of the New World, Taxation without Representation, and all that. Hence, leading this thing we now call the United States of America. The Boston Tea Party and all that stuff.

Anyway, I am pretty sure that Britain and its other empires cleaned out a lot of their excess of prisoners in those locations and decided to sell them off to the colonies rather than keep them up in prisons and other locations. At this time Britain had control over a lot of countries and continents. They were quite a bit over-extended I would say. That is why they lost control of this "New World".

So, prisoners were sold to the colonies, others sought passage to this new world and basically sold themselves as indentured servants of whatever. If you give me passage to this new world, I will work for you for X amount of time. My guess would be that there were people of all creeds, colors, and races that sought to make a better life in this new world and others that had no choice. Slavery is slavery and laborers and laborers, right? If I/We need help, who cares what they look like.

I guess my first point is that slaves were not just any single color, race or creed. My guess would be that many human entities in the US today can trace their ancestry back to some of these people brought over on these ships against their will, as slaves, indentured servants, etc. It wasn't just a plague thrust upon the Black population that is pushed upon us today. Some of our relatives were on those same ships under those same conditions. It just makes more sense to me.

Now, that isn't to say that some unscrupulous human entities did not go out of their way to massively exploit the Black population by going to other countries for the sole purpose of begging, borrowing, trading, and stealing multiples of thousands of Black human entities for the sole purpose of selling them at the docks to be human laborers and slaves for the colonies of this new found world. That has surely been proven many times over! I am sure the amounts of Black entities surely outweighed the amounts of other entities affected by this plight! Although, any other colors would have surely been taken for granted. Give credit where credit is due. Slavery affected all colors, races, and or creeds.

At this point we know slavery has entered this new world. When I think of this new world, I think of what the eastern coast of the US is now. So, these ship loads of laborers for sale stretch from the north and south coast. I could only guess that there were slaves in every area of that stretch, north and south. Then we have expansion, expanding from the east to the west. I'm not going to pry into the east to west expansion. It could have little to do with my topic here, but my predominant topic here is slavery and the Civil War, which would be the north and the south.

When you talk about the Civil War you mostly talk about northeast and southeast not northwest and southwest. That is a whole other piece of injustice. Injustice against the Natives that were here in this land before any of our ancestors arrived and made them move on to their so-called reservations. That may be another topic for me to think too deeply about.

So, we have decided that we now have slaves throughout the northeastern and southeastern colonies. We have decided that these colonies have now broken away from British rule. This new world now has been called the United States of America. A lot has happened in a relatively short amount of time. When you look at the rest of the world that is.

Slavery has been going on for many years within this new world called the USA. Abraham Lincoln was the sixteenth president. So, slavery was an okay and acceptable practice under 15 presidents. What led this new president to be an opponent of slavery? There is a lot of conjecture here, let us just say that he was and leave it at that as his reasoning may have been additional factors other than just his own. Maybe there were some political or other reasons? Sometimes others can sway our thinking.

One of the things my earlier professor mentioned was expansion. That expansion was the main reason for the Civil War and that the end of slavery was a reason but not the main primer of tensions and hostilities. Tension and hostilities against the south. That kind of makes sense if you know a lot of history within the US and this thing is called expansion. There was a massive expansion from east to west, at an almost unbelievable scale. Could it not make sense that this could also involve and cause further expansion from north to south? The north which was stronger and had a larger more willing population than its weaker area within the south.

When I think of the Civil War I think of the eastern half of the US. Yes, there were California, Nevada and Oregon, who sided with the north, but I don't recall massive battles or hostilities within those states. Let's just talk about expansion. I guess that expansion is relative to where the actual slave populations were. When you compare the north and the south it is like there were two brothers, the bigger brother was called north and he was like the actor John Wayne, bigger and larger than life. Then there was the smaller brother the Al Pacino, smaller in size but had a big presence. At that time the north (Union) had a free population of 22 million and a slave population of 90 thousand. The south (Confederacy) at that time had a free population of 6 million and slave population of 3 million. War statistics count around 2 million soldiers for the union and 1 million for the confederacy.

I can surely see the bigger brother picking on the smaller brother and taking his toy away from him. If he only had a reason? A reason to be a big bully? During that time, what would be the reasoning to cause such strife between these two brothers? After all they were brothers, right? The war was brother against brother, right? Could or would the sole ideology of slavery be a reason for brother to kill brother or could there be additional powers at play here?

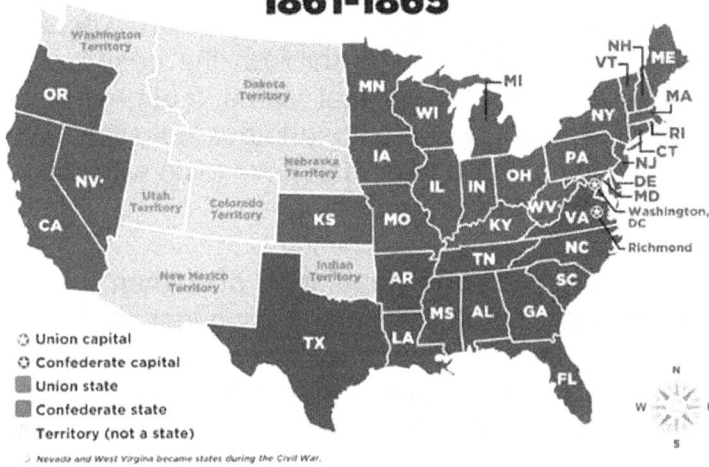

The Civil War
1861-1865

Washington Territory
OR
Dakota Territory
MN
MI
WI
NV·
Utah Territory
Colorado Territory
Nebraska Territory
IA
IL
IN
OH
PA
NH
VT
ME
MA
NY
RI
CT
NJ
DE
MD
Washington, DC
CA
New Mexico Territory
KS
MO
KY
WV
VA
Richmond
Indian Territory
AR
TN
NC
MS
AL
GA
SC
TX
LA
FL

○ Union capital
◌ Confederate capital
▨ Union state
▨ Confederate state
   Territory (not a state)

☽ Nevada and West Virgina became states during the Civil War.

N
W   E
S

When I look at the Civil War and the states involved, I think about expansion.

The north: I see 7 states in the north are land-locked and border with Canada. I see 9 that are water-front property. I see 5 that are land-locked that border the southern states involved in the Civil War.

The south: I see 1 state in the south is land-locked and borders with Mexico. I see 9 that are water-front property. I see 3 that are land-locked that border the northern states involved in the Civil War.

I see California and the New Mexico Territory which are not really in the hostilities and are also land-locked with Mexico, although California also has water-front property as well as Oregon.

Think about this…

I don't know how many years I have heard that the rich man starts the wars, and the poor man fights them. I can't say how many war movies I have seen where you have the soldiers trudging through the desert or the swamp and expressing that same thought. Is that correct? This brings me to another question. What does a rich man or a poor man have to do with slavery, either continuing it or abolishing it?

Will the plight of one population of human cause a brother to kill a brother? Here is my question. It is true at this time the slave color we are discussing is Black and there are 3 million of those being held captive in the south. Would knowing this trial and tribulation of the Black slaves cause a divide in a family that has no real relationship nor has possibly never seen a Black slave in the first place? Does that make sense? Could I actively go into a battle and participate in the killing of my neighbor, friend, and or brother for an idea? That is my question? Is that real, or is there more to stake than meets the eye or was there more to the propaganda machine of that time to persuade brother to kill brother?

In my mind: Like I tell my students. For a human entity to get involved in something you must make something personal for them. Most people do not get involved with something, or fight for something, unless it immediately affects them. It must be made personal for them, especially, for something as drastic as a neighbor or brother to fight or kill one another. I would think generally not and that there must be some massive propaganda machine driving these hostilities.

When you are driving down south you see prison road gangs sometimes chained together beside the road either cleaning or working. Could you pull up alongside the guard and kill him to let those prisoners go free? They are held hostage and captive against their will. I know that is a bit far-fetched, but this is to make you think. Well, think.

How about this: You are getting older, and your eyes and hands don't quite work as good as they once did. You are a watch maker by trade. This profession involves very intricate work. One day you are out walking around and you hear an auctioneer. It is new to you, and you walk over to see what is happening. You see they are selling people. You have heard of this, but you have never really witnessed it in person. It is legal and pretty much a normal thing to do this. You know others in your neighborhood or area that own people. It is just a new thought to you. You have a small amount of cash in your pocket. It is just a spur of the moment thought.

You watch for a time and most of the entities being reviewed and sold are larger and full of muscle. These seem to be the prime candidates. Then this rather small, frail entity is brought forth. They mention several traits of this person, and he fits the mold that you once fit as a watch maker. Then the thought takes you over. "I have a little money, and I could teach this person my craft and he could help me". "I can't spend all my cash, but could this be a good investment to help me further help my family?" It never even crosses your mind that this is slavery, as that probably isn't really a word of that day and time in the first place, after all, it is an acceptable and moral practice,

It appears no one is bidding on the candidate, so your small purse is accepted. You now are the proud owner of a helper for you and your family.

You bring him in, you clothe him, shelter him, feed him and teach him. He is a tremendous help. You have turned him into a younger version of you. He does what you can no longer do. You feel you cannot express to him enough how he has helped you! He knows how you feel, and you know how he feels about you and your family! This is NOT to say that ALL slaves were treated this way as I know the majority were NOT!

Now the decision throughout the land is that slavery is immoral and must be abolished. What do you do? How do you think? What do you think? What does your slave think? He is a slave you know; you hold his papers. He is your bought and paid for property. Does your mindset now change toward him? He has done nothing wrong to you! The surroundings are pushing this new-found ideal. If I am to give him his freedom, what will happen to me and my family, he is our whole support? What do I do?

To make a long story short. To give it a realistic ending. This once frail entity has now thrived because of the small amount of money you spent. He had nothing when he was sold and now has things he could have never acquired if you had left him to who-knows what kind of life. He has always been grateful to you and you to him. You decide to give him his freedom. You feel it is only the right thing to do. You sign and give him his papers. You realize it will be a struggle for you and your family, but it is your and their will.

Now, thoughts abound. Thoughts from you and your family and thoughts from your newly freed slave. Now that I am free, what do I do, where do I go? It is easy to be free and say you are free and have papers that are signed and say you are free, but are you really free? Is anyone really free? We must think back at that day and time. These are realistic questions and there would be very few realistic answers.

The newly freed slave could walk two miles down the road and be taken as a slave once again. He would present his papers, and they would surely be torn up or burned in front of his eyes. What could this man do? Nothing at that point. He may or may not have any idea of his ancestry at that time. Even if he knew where he came from it would be a massive undertaking to try and resume to that location. I would guess he would do what the majority of those newly freed slaves would do at that time. He would stay or try to stay where he is. At least there is some form of safety and security.

If there were in fact 3 million slaves in the south and 90 thousand in the north, where do you go when you are all of a sudden freed? Talk about a massive exodus. This would have been one. Where do you go? What do you do? Suddenly you are free and no one has any responsibility for you in any way, shape or form.

What many of those apparently did, were to stay where they were and became share-croppers on the same plantations they were slaves on. The owners of those fields had to have workers to produce or there would be no money transferring. I guess it may have been free room and board for work. Then came the carpetbaggers from the north to take advantage of the land owners of the south. What do you do when you have acres and acres with no laborers to work them?

Well, how about this? Did the northern interest really extend to the south? If this was for expansion from the north to the south, where is the information of industry taking over the south? Moving the southern population from their homelands and letting industry take those lands over. I don't really know of any. However, what many don't realize is: At that time there were non-state territories that lie inside the western half of the US at that time, and those large tracts of land were where southern interests were trying to expand the south to the west and bring slave labor with them. That might be the expansion that was discussed and later crushed.

So, apparently the salve labor driven economy of the south was being used to gain expansion in the west through the same slave labor that was used throughout the south for many years. Now things are starting to make sense. The same slave labor that was making only a certain population of southern landowners richer and richer. Their only interest was to make themselves richer and richer through the use of slave labor. I guess why we did not see a mass of slave labor out west was because that plan was thwarted through the efforts of the north winning the Civil War.

So, this slave expansion toward the western territories was still a major reason and cause of the civil hostilities. Expansion of the west is the culprit, but the tool was the slave labor. Now that makes more sense. So, I think I can honestly say that the end of the Civil War did in fact bring about the end of slavery within the USA.

Now, the end of slavery does not mean that there will be a sudden shift to equality for everyone. The intention was to free slaves. It was not to free slaves and give them equal rights. It may have been thought that way, and that the winning of the war by the north might cause some form of shift, but I think that was a far-fetched idea within itself, as we all know it took another hundred years to bring up the subject of equality.

Was it an end to slavery or the end of some form or forms of oppression?

Girls and Boys

I remember a joke about a girl and a guy on a picnic in the woods. The girl complains that every time she has to urinate, she squats down and scratches her behind on the briars. Then the guy stands up, pulls out his "handy gadget" and freely urinates standing up. The girl then says, "that's a handy gadget to bring on a picnic".

I am not a biblical scholar by any means. Everyone always points to the Bible and expects everyone on the planet to follow its divine advice. Everyone points to it and says they use it as a guide, but if that were the fact, in all truthfulness, there would be less sin. I cannot imagine a world with less sin than we have today. It seems to grow daily. I guess that is the sin of mankind. The sin of mankind was brought about by the Adam and Eve situation. We all heard the story. What did I hear last week? That there was new light in relation to religion and that Eve has a chance of being resurrected as she was deceived by the snake and the Devil and that Adam has no chance of being resurrected as he was not deceived, he knew better than to take the bite.

Anyway, there are girls and boys. There are girls born with boy parts I hear tell, and there are boys born with girl parts. I don't know if that makes you any less of a human entity or being, that is just how the cards were dealt out, as we are still under the sin of mankind. The luck of the draw, I guess. Playing the cards that are dealt to you.

I don't know if the issue is that girls want to have the right to urinate and have bowel movements in front of boys or vice versa. I doubt that, in all reality. All I can say is I am 60 years old, and I don't care who is looking as if I have to go, I have to go! I can, however, understand if I was younger, that I probably would not care for it.

I can't imagine a girl wanting to compete against a boy and vice versa. Who wants to compete when you may have an advantage, then it really isn't a fair competition? Who wants to win that way? Don't you want to compete and win through your own merit with like-minded and statured people like yourself? It just sems odd to me. Do you have moral fiber and compass? It would just seem unfair, and I would want no part of knowing I won that way. But that is me, and not everyone is like me.

A G o o d L e a d e r

A leader is only as good as the people under him/her. You can be as rich as you want to be, but money does not make you a good leader. If this human entity has vaults of money, you can bet that there are people under that person who are the smart ones. The truly smart leader has smart ones under him/her to help make the decisions. You can bet that each good or great President of the United States had a good or great cabinet under them that assisted them in making wise choices and decisions.

Sometimes, we think in our minds we can stand alone, but in fact maybe not. Someone who is thought of as a good or great leader may soon run out of gas if they do not have a good or great team under them.

F r i e n d s

Do you have friends? Do you really have friends? Hold your hand out, spread your fingers and count how many you have. Better yet, count up how many you think you have. What is a friend anyway? Just someone you ran into one time or a neighbor down the road you wave at when you drive by. I'm not talking about those human entities; those are not your real friends. First, we need to define a friend. To me a friend is someone who will watch out for me. Someone who will watch my back. Someone who I can count on when the times get tough. Someone who will stand fast and tell me when they think or know I am doing something I don't need to be doing. Someone who will say "Look stupid, you don't need to be doing that! I am your friend and stop!" That to me is a friend. A real friend!

Do you have one of those?

Really, do you?

I see celebrities on the news all the time that get caught for doing something stupid! Maybe they had more money than brains? Did they have a true friend anywhere on the planet that had the caring to sit them down and say, "Look stupid......."? I really doubt it. Isn't that what a friend is for? They are not really judging you; they are just trying to guide and sway you from doing something they deem is not in your best interest or something that puts you in a bad light! That is just one side of being a friend, mentally looking out for you.

Another friend is the person who looks out for you, physically. Several years ago, there was this girl who went on a spring break to some other country. She came up missing and they never found her. It was all over the news. She supposedly had friends with her on this venture to another country. In my opinion, she had no friends, or this would not have happened, and she would be with us today. How could anyone at that time stand up and say they were her friend when they did not watch out for her and let her come up missing. I cannot even imagine speaking or even acknowledging any single one of them as her friend! She had no true friends with her when she left the United States and she had no true friends when she was here! Shameful!

Just a few weeks ago the same thing happened to another girl. Another girl who went to another country with her supposed friends and now she is missing. Here we are once again. A friend would leave the party with the friend they came with! A friend would know where their friend was! Are you kidding me? You claim to have been my friend, and you left me to the wolves? What right do you have to claim to be my friend? This is unbelievable to me!

I remember when I was younger, a lot of my friends and I rented a chalet in Gatlinburg. One night a bunch decide to go down the mountain to town and walk around. Later that day, after dark they came back and we had a party, twenty or so of us. I stayed on the mountain that day for some reason. Anyway, the party went on and on for hours. About three in the morning, we all had enough and went to bed. Several hours later one of my friends came in the front door alone and was mad! Did he have a right to be mad?

The friends he went down the mountain with lost track of him and came back up the mountain without him. Our chalet was about a mile straight up the mountain through the woods. He could hear the partying and see all the lights of our party but the roads were winding up the mountain, so he just went straight up hiking through the woods. It was quite a few hours of a journey trekking through the weeds and woods. I would have been mad too!

I always heard growing up, "You should leave the party with who you came with". Seems like a wise decision to me. I would hope someone was looking out for me, watching my back, and letting me know when I was out of line.

H e l l

I know some religions believe there is a heaven and a hell, and some do not. All I have to say is I see some of the things people do to other people and animals. I sincerely hope there is a hell as some of these human entities need to go there. "Go directly to hell, do not pass go, and do not receive $200 dollars!

However, I remember my dad always saying that in the old days farmers said they put potatoes in Hell and that meant they turned them under the ground.

Just a Job

There is an old song lyric "Calling it your job old Hoss sure don't make it right". There are many jobs on this planet taken by human elements that get a paycheck for their time. Many jobs I would not care to do and many that the sheer inner nature of my being and sanity would not allow me to do. If I wanted to live without guilt that is. I'm not talking about the things human elements do in the name of God, King, and Country. In a movie, Harry Brown, Caine and his friend were sitting in a pub talking about old times gone by. His friend asked him if he ever killed anyone in the war? Caine said, "You cannot ask me that, I was a different person then". Anyway, I am not talking about those things.

I'm talking about the dirty jobs some people do and seem to have no conscience. As long as they are getting paid, I suspect. Do you know how veal cattle are treated before they end up in a package at the store? Have you ever been to the stockyard and watched the baby pigs play together? How about dairy cows? Do they roam free until they get milked? How about a new one, Kobe or Wagyu cattle? Are they fed alcohol and given massages to keep their beef tender? I believe the native Americans in this country had it right, they killed and ate only what they needed to survive and generally gave thanks the ultimate provider for giving that other animals life to them.

How about some things we don't eat. Do you think a rodeo bull just hangs out in a field all day and just gets mean? Mean enough to put on a big show for the crowd. What is his reward? The chopping block when he tires of performing. Have you ever heard of a horse breed called a Tennessee Walker? How does it keep its tail raised up so high? That looks painful. Have you ever watched a video of dogs being euthanized at a dog shelter when they never get chosen to go home with a family? I guess we survive by turning our heads. I often turn my head in shame.

No Cure

Do we realize how much money revolves around things we would like to see a cure for? Take for instance cancer. I have never thought I could be thought of as being naïve. I have always figured there would never be a cure for cancer. I have never thought there would be a cure for crime. Think about the number of people on the earth today that survive by working in fields of medical and law enforcement. Prisons and medical facilities are being built all the time. Grant money is devoted every year. Curing cancer would put a lot of people out of work. So would law enforcement. We would like to see it happen, but I doubt we ever will. I know that isn't being very positive, but I am a realist.

Death Penalty

I may be old fashioned, but I think if DNA proves you to be guilty beyond a shadow of a doubt you should reap the consequences. If you ran over someone with a vehicle 15 times you need to be run over by a vehicle 15 times. If you raped someone then you murdered them by stabbing them 17 times, well, I think I have said what I want to say. I don't see a reason for death row in a prison. Go to court, get proven guilty, take you to a special place, and end it! Why should taxpayers pay the bill? Do something positive with that expense. Feed and shelter the homeless.

Your Choice

I recently read where a younger male who was a citizen of the United States, packed his bags, moved to another country and enlisted in their military. He was captured by the enemy of that country. His family who are citizens of the USA are wanting the USA to step in and call for his release. I think he chose his path. It didn't sound like a very well thought out plan, so you reap what you sew. I try not to make quick decisions. But hey, as long as you accept the consequences, it is your choice. Life is full of choices, I would suggest taking out a piece of paper and making a column for pros and a column for cons and weigh them out.

Country Hate

I always wonder if leaders or people of other countries think at all. Does their opinions of the USA sway from day to day? Today they like us and tomorrow they may not. What is the deal anyway?

Why is it always the Good Ole USA that always steps in and saves the day? I am sure it isn't as simple as that but ask our military people what they think. They are the ones on the ground sent in to save the day. Cemeteries are filled with veterans that gave all to save others. Others not just Americans but others from all around the world.

Russia should have nothing bad to say about the US. If it wasn't for the US stepping in during WWII there would not be a Russia as we know it today. It was being taken out by Germany and Hitler. We don't hear much hate coming from Italy, maybe they are grateful to the US? They were also on Hitler's list. China is always complaining! If it wasn't for the US during WWII China would be under the stern hand of Japan. Japan wasn't too far from taking them over. What about Africa? During WWII how many countries were traversing through that country with speed? Remember the Afrika Corps from Germany? Britain surely must remember what was about to happen to them during WWII and other engagements. Japan and Germany may have been small countries but look at what they accomplished and could have accomplished. I'm not even going to go into the middle east and the far east. I am probably just wasting my breath.

Very few countries have a right to hate the USA. They want to hate us because we don't, won't and either slow down on buying the "low-priced disposable" crap that comes from their country. Is that the problem we have with the US? Should we keep our own people up!

I guess that is the price we pay in the US because we don't make much within our country anymore. Well, I don't know what the limit is or the stopping point. We need to take care of ourselves. I know, logistics, logistics, logistics. It would seem to me that after we take care of ourselves then we would be in a more prosperous place to reach out and help others.

What Rights

What are these rights we all hear about and think we have? I only really am aware of three: to live, pay taxes and die.

I hear people scream all the time about the Constitution and the rights it provides. I do not believe that is correct. The Bill of Rights provides the rights not the Constitution. The Constitution is the base that points to who is accountable. I remember when I was a kid there were cartoons on TV that talked about these things, and I have not seen them for many years. "I'm just a Bill on Capitol Hill". Are those cartoons still relevant today? I would think so, as those things have not changed, supposedly.

There were cartoons for English writing. Remember "Conjunction Junction what's your Function" back then it was called Schoolhouse Rock. Cartoons that taught you something. Cartoons back in those days seemed to try and teach kids something. I remember a lot of them today.

Back to these rights we think we have. The Bill of Rights grants us rights, inalienable rights that is. Oh no, now I am confusing this with the Declaration of Independence. I better not do that. I am not trying for myself to secede from the United States and make myself my own country or state. We already did that. That was a major pain.

Whatever rights you think you have, make sure you stand up and take responsibility for your actions. You have the right to be as smart as you think you are and as dumb as you think you need to be. You may be asked to pay a price from those actions. You have that right.

E m i n e n t   D o m a i n

Quite a few years back one of my roommates after college mentioned he wanted to invest in some real estate. It was several years after my flight school years, and he was already a successful pilot for a major airline. He made quite a large amount of money and wanted to invest. As he was an airline pilot, he had traveled throughout all the territories owned by the United States.

He was interested in Puerto Rico as it was a United States Territory and Costa Rica, but Costa Rico was not a territory of the USA.

My friend mentioned at that time there were many investment opportunities in those areas off the Caribbean Ocean. He talked about how beautiful the beaches, the coastline, waterfalls, cliffs, etc.

He said there were some things he needed to research first. One of the things was that they were now allowing non-citizens to purchase property. The purchaser would buy the property, have it put into and deeded to their name. The purchaser would then be the owner of the property and could build on that property. The purchaser would then be responsible for taking care of that property that was in their name. The problem my friend had while researching was, he said that the property was always really owned by the government of that country, but the country was allowing citizens and non-citizens to own that property.

His thoughts were confusing to me. Was my friend really this ignorant of property possession, the rules and regulations of owning property? Did he not understand how to buy and sell property? Maybe he needed a lesson? Maybe he needed to understand how it is outside of the USA as he had never researched laws around the rest of the world.

Anyway..............................

In the United States of America, the government owns the rights to all property within their boundary. Are you getting this? The US government owns all the physical dirt and water within the USA. The US government issues deeds to property. Your grandma, grandpa, mom, and or dad may hold a title or deed to a piece of property. That deed is in their name and valid. They may "own" that property.

What exactly does "own" mean? Own means that the deed or title is in the holder's name and documented. By owning the holder is responsible for the upkeep and taking care of that property. In most states within the USA the owner of that property pays taxes on that property every year. That means the holder pays taxes to own that piece of property each year and the holder takes care of that piece of property each year.

How about an example: There is a term called Eminent Domain. You might want to look that up. Eminent Domain means the government has the power to take your deeded or titled property from you or re-use a portion of that titled or deeded property any time it sees fit. For instance, if the state, county, or city wants to put a road through the middle of your property for some reason, they can go through a process and take your property, buy it, or whatever they deem necessary. It happens and you may not really hear about it. It is the same with zoning and re-zoning of existing property. Cities, counties and states do it all the time. They hold meetings where they invite the public to come and share their thoughts, but in the end these boards of administrators already have made plans to carry out whatever they propose they just play the game by inviting the public to share their thoughts. Then the board passes and approves what they were going to pass in the first place, before you even came to say what you wanted to say.

How about another example: We are all human beings, and we think nothing bad will ever happen to us. Right? Until it does. What if you own a piece of property and a section of it, you decide you are not going to mow it for some reason? Depending upon the location of that property you may receive a notice from the city or county telling you to mow it. Telling you that you are responsible for the upkeep. If you say, well it is my property, I will do what I want with it, and I am not going to mow it. You may come home one day, and someone either has or is mowing it. Do not worry; you will get a bill in the mail for that service. They warned you and you did not heed their advice.

How about another example: Since we think, nothing will ever happen to us. What if you have some property in your name and you forget or do not pay taxes on it for one year. You will hopefully get some notices in the mail. If you do not pay those taxes, your property will come up for sale on the courthouse steps. Whoever pays the taxes on it may have it put into their name and you may need to find another place to live.

How about another example: You own a house, which is on a piece of property. You suddenly go into the hospital. You die that night. You do not have a will expressing whom your property goes to. You are dead. In some instances, the government may seek out your living relatives. Do they have to seek them out? I do not think so. The government does not want your property anyway! All they want is for someone to pay taxes on it every year and keep it up. If there is no extended family to leave the property to, it reverts to the government, city and or state.

In fact, you pay taxes every year to have a title or deed for property to be in your name. You can legally hand it down from generation to generation if that is your desire. However, if it is forgotten or left unmaintained it will most likely revert back to the city and state government for resale.

Therefore, when you drive around to a neighborhood or through a city and you see a piece of property that looks condemned or out of care. If it is still not in the name of the city or county to be sold or torn down. Someone or some entity owns that title or deed and is paying the taxes on it.

It is kind of like rent-to-own, and follow the rules or it goes back to the government. Is it that all they want is for you to pay the taxes and take care of that property until they, the government, finds a use for it and they need it more than you do.

P r o f i l i n g

Profiling is kind of like a bulleted description or sketch. Profiling is a prolific or creative form of labeling. Labeling with an exhaustive list of traits. We see a lot these days on TV and on the news about profiling. If YOU do some research, YOU will see that pretty much all law enforcement entities use profiling to catch the bad guy. The FBI, CIA, DHS, NCI, and ATF are some of these entities. Some human entities spend years of their lives learning how to profile and how to examine proof to put together profiles. Profiling saves lives. I'm not going to reach out here and give an opinion as to whether or not the pros of profiling far outweigh the cons. This isn't my place. The reason I write these assignments is for YOU to review and give YOUR opinions.

Social media is much more prominent in our current times than it was 20/30 years ago. It is in-your-face and available everywhere. You see things presented and published today that would not have even been a thought or available back then. Good or bad it is here!

However, I do think sometimes law enforcement gets a bad rap overall. Yes, I will agree there are bad apples around many corners, but I think YOU cannot blame all of law enforcement for the issues with some of them.

Have YOU ever watched a TV show called Andy Griffith, from the 1960s? This was a popular show that came on each week about a small-town Sheriff, his deputy and his family. It must have been popular it was on for eight years and is still on some TV channels today. Then there was another show that ran from 1968 to 1975 called Adam-12. A show about two Police officers in a Metro City environment.

I graduated high school in 1982. During the next ten or so years I got to know quite a few Police officers. Several of the guys I went to elementary, junior and high school became Police officers. If any of YOU are old enough to remember back during those times every Police car in the US had a sticker on it. That sticker said, "To Serve and To Protect." If YOU can remember that far back? That was the thinking of the law enforcement personnel at that time. As a matter of fact, when I was younger in a small town, if myself and or my buddies were out doing something we should not be doing, the local police would follow us home or take us home. They would tell us to stay home, and they did not want to see us back out again tonight!

What changed? What changed in the mentality of the law enforcement personnel? Then, all of a sudden, we did not see the sticker on vehicles anymore. The stickers were now removed and nonexistent. What changed this? I'll tell YOU what changed the way of thinking that had been so prominent for all of law enforcement. The thinking that law enforcement was there to be helping hand to the people. War is what happened!

When wars end what happens to the military participants? Most of the ones who are not killed or wounded come back to their old towns looking for work.

Also, since crime goes up every year and never seems to go down there are always available law enforcement positions open and available. For a person who has spent years and or multiple deployments providing security and or a form of law enforcement throughout the world, where do YOU think they might be applicable to find a position or job? That's right, the law enforcement sector. Some local law enforcement personnel might wear the old school beige/brown uniforms but most of the time YOU see tactical gear and BDUs (Battle Dress Uniforms) either camouflage or solid colors. That didn't happen by accident.

The dress (uniform) brings the mentality and or the mentality defines the dress. That is what happened! To serve and protect changed!

More Profiling

Back when I was younger you could get on a bus, airplane, etc. with a gun. I remember every semester I would take a train from Savannah Georgia to Fort Meyers Florida to stay with my grandparents over the summer. I would always take along one of my shotguns. I would have it on a soft case and take it on the train with my other bag. It has been many years since something like that was permissible to happen.

On another note: I remember when I was in the 8th grade in North Little Rock Arkansas in Junior High School we had a show-and-tell one day. Each student brought something from their home related to their family history to class and explained it to the other students and their teacher. My great grandfather was in the Civil War on the side of the Union. He was involved in what was later called "The Great Train Robbery". He and several other men in his company and several spies store a Confederate train called the "General". They drove the train from the south and headed up north destroying southern things along the way. Anyway, my grandfather was the 6th man to receive the Congressional Medal of Honor (CMH). Matter of fact, the first batch of CMH medals were given to these men along with my grandfather. The sword that my grandfather was presented as a part of the CMH award was the family relic I took to the show-and-tell. I got into trouble for bringing a weapon on that school campus.

One of these stories goes one way and the other story goes the other way. This is why I mention them. My guess, as of today, I doubt very seriously you would get away with taking any form of a weapon on a train, bus, etc. or be able to take any sort of similar item to a show-and-tell on a physical school campus.

These stories bring me to the topic of this writing "profiling".

My riding the train story when I was 18 or 19 years old. Then my show-and-tell story when I was 13 years old.

Question: In the first story, I was around 18 years of age. At that time or even currently what 18-year-old white kid has carried out a mass shooting on a train using a shotgun?

Question: In the second story, I was around 13 years of age. At that time or even currently what 13-year-old white kid has carried out a mass stabbing in a school classroom with a sword?

You could call this a type of profiling.

Maybe a little more explanation. Let us reverse the reality!

In the first story: Let us say I was an 18-year-old white kid, and I murdered everyone on the train with the shotgun I had brought with me.

So, would you think it be normal to look and review every 18-year-old white kid carrying a shotgun on your train before boarding? As he might be a potential threat.

In the second story: Let us say I was a 13-year-old white kid and I murdered everyone in my classroom with the sword I brought to class for show-and-tell.

So, would you think it be normal to look and review every 13-year-old white kid carrying a sword to class? As he might be a potential threat.

It seems a bit far-fetched but think about it.

By profiling the past and seeing that, it was an 18 and a 13-year-old white kid that perpetrated these murders. These two would be subject to more scrutiny when trying to board trains and enter classrooms because the past history PROVES this point. This is proof! This is profiling.

Another profiling example:

You may not realize this. Have you ever heard of 9-11? When the airplanes flew into the twin towers in New York City and killed many people. Look it up.

Well, 9-11 caused a LOT of profiling at airports. I mean a lot of profiling that never existed before. Who were the people who got onto these airplanes at the airports? What was their nationality? What did they look like? How were they dressed? They were all men and no women. None of them was White and none of them was Black. They were all lighter skinned but darker than white. They were all of the same nationality. Right after 9-11 happened if you went to airports, you would see the people that fit the physical descriptions of all those who participated in the 9-11 tragedy were detained at airports MORE than anyone else. They were taken aside and put through a more rigorous boarding process than any other persons.

Question: If you were getting ready to be on an airplane would you feel safer knowing that some of those passengers were detained and made 100% sure they would not harm you or take over the plane once it took off and maybe kill you and everyone else on board, or do you not really care and are willing to take the chance that those people are safe? But we all know there is no such thing as 100% safety and security, but would this use of profiling not make it at least a higher level of safety than 50%? Does that make sense?

We all want to be safe. Right? As safe as we want to feel we are anyway.

Now, I can see both sides of a profiling issue. You will always have exceptions to every rule. Every person at that airport being screened twice does not have to be a terrorist. Every person at that airport dressed the same way as those 9-11 terrorists does not have to be a terrorist. Every person at that airport that is the same nationality does not nor will all of them be terrorists.

Would you rather be safe than sorry because you did not double-check some of those people who fit the same profile as the 9-11 terrorists that killed all those people?

This is a HUGE topic that covers a lot of ground.

In my opinion. If we can save one single life through profiling and being more cautious than it is worth the inconvenience of anyone within a society. We all have to help as it is the responsibility of all of us as a whole.

Now, that said there is another side effect of profiling.

Does or can it bring about detainment and false imprisonment and incarceration for someone just because of their race or creed. You bet it can. It happens all the time and probably every day. I cannot say this enough; there are good cops and there are bad cops. You cannot have a 100% secure and credible law enforcement force. That does not exist. Anything that is 100% does not exist. You will always have that, I am afraid. You will always have an element of conjecture. I do not care where you are. Nothing is ever 100%.

How about one last scenario. When I was around 22 years old there was a rash of destruction at the local town cemetery. Someone had been going into the cemetery at night breaking headstones, moving markers and stones around. The cemetery gates closed and locked at 8 pm at night but you could walk to just about everywhere around the cemetery and gain entrance, as there was no real fence around it. The cemetery was in the middle of town and many neighborhoods backed up to the cemetery grounds. It was concluded that kids were probably going in there and damaging those things.

The local law enforcement decided that the probable profile of the ones doing the damage were kids or teenagers on foot who may even live in one of the neighborhoods adjacent to the cemetery. For the next week law enforcement took the names down of every kid or teenager they saw walking around the area between the hours of 8 pm at night and until the cemetery opened each morning. By following, this profiling the damage within the cemetery stopped after the first week. This was a positive profiling.

Springer Reality

Have you ever watched the television show Jerry Springer? I like to think of it as a reality show. The show where guests are invited to share their life experiences, then the audience gets to ask questions, then Jerry gives his final thought.

It seems every time I am turning through the channels this show grabs me and pulls me in and I just have to continue watching until the end, the final thought. It isn't the crazy titles of each episode of the topics; it is the realism of the show. It takes me back to the premise that babies are born knowing nothing and the relationships they go through during their lives and the positive and negative contacts they make, make them who they are today.

It really does not surprise me, as the older I get, the less surprised I am at anything! It does not surprise me the thoughts, ideas, concepts, and ideals that the guests play host to. The human entities that see their ways as normal and they often fight for the rights they believe to be normal. That is why I watch the show. I guess I like to see how the "other half" lives so-to-speak. I like to think I am somewhat normal, although who is to say what is and what is not normal in this day and time? What is normal anyway? Some say "tomato", and some say "tomato".

I don't live my life around episodes of the Jerry Springer show, although I mention it to make a point. The point being: In real life, each day, in our lives, whether it is at work or at home or doing our daily routines we will run into people who we think "just don't get the point". Sometimes you can draw a picture and give a long-drawn-out explanation, and they still do not understand what you are getting at. Sometimes you can write out in detail with black ink on a piece of white paper and they still don't get the point! It is right there in front of them and you get so frustrated! You just want to stand up and shout "what is your malfunction?" It can be so frustrating that you just want to pull your hair out, or theirs.

I run into this so often. You cannot say it is the blind leading the blind. Sometimes even the most technological and detailed of explanations still don't seem to "bring the point home". Everyone always seems to be of the opinion that there is always some terrestrial entity that safeguards and there are some behind the scenes checks-and-balances that are going on. I have always been one of those people that can listen to and watch a speaker and read between the lines of what he or she is actually saying. I can see what he or she is actually saying that the others are not grasping. They are not grasping the full content or context of their explanation. I most certainly always grasp it. I would guess that my past life history and upbringing allow me to see what others do not. Most people are garish and will actually tell you their plan if you really listen. Most human elements think they are above others and think you will not pay attention to what they say, so you just need to open your ears and pay attention.

Example: One of the educational facilities I had worked had a high-level administrator who said he was a religious man. He had given many sermons during his years and was a high-level entity within his religious place of worship. This human entity would give eloquent speeches and professed to be a leader of all that was right, true and honest. During his speeches he would often get the "Amen" and shouts from the audience multiple times throughout his performance. It sometimes felt like a circus performance with the praising, clapping and audience participation. You could look around at the crowd and notice the non-believers in the audience that just wanted it all to end. It was like they knew it was a false profit opining or at least a profit spreading falsities.

Long story short: The profit had a prolific downfall from grace. He was found out, eventually. A whistleblower brought him down to his knees.

After the downfall the buzz of discussion around was "how did this happen as there are check-and-balances? Where were the checks-and-balances? Who were the checks-and-balances? How could this happen? The outcome of all the questions seemed to point out: What better human entity to fleece-the-flock than the upstanding religious entity that praised himself as being pious and full of grace?

I was walking and talking one day with one of my peers and she asked me how could someone who professed to be an upstanding and religious person lie, steal and cheat? The person who was asking was quite religious. She did not understand how a person who claimed to be one thing and was found out to be really something else. She seemed to be somewhat lost, and I guess she had been relatively sheltered from the realisms of today. I mentioned to her "what better person to deceive others than the one you perceive that would not deceive". That is the entity that will get you every time. "Ask Adam what happened to him?"

Education for Everyone

What is education anyway? Dictionaries define education as the giving and or receiving of systematic instruction. They further add especially at a school or university. Prior to dictionaries, what would we consider education? What would a caveman consider as education prior to schools or universities? How did the extension of schools and or universities come to get added to the single word, education? Why do we make everything so complicated?

To me education is learning to do anything. Standing beside my dad with the hood of the car up and handing him tools or watching him change the station wagon tire beside the freeway with cars buzzing past. That is to me education. Learning to do something/anything that I had either not have done before or I had done before but was researching how to maybe do it better the next time. That is education to me.

So, when I say everyone needs an education, that is what I mean. Everyone needs an education or to be educated. Educated in some manner! Education could be as simple as reconciling a check register, or cooking a favorite Sunday after religious services lunch, brunch, or dinner. That is education to me. Either someone physically showing someone how to do something or someone researching and or learning themselves. Everyone needs an education.

Does everyone need to go to school? Does everyone need to go to college? Does everyone need to go to university? My answer would be a solid no! Do people realize the number of jobs open within my country, the United States today that are available with little to no education? Hundreds of thousands published and hundreds of thousands I am sure of non-published. Just walk down one of the business streets in your town and see how many wanted signs are on the doors. Just in case you have not been out in a while. You will surely be surprised or maybe not.

I remember when I was 16 years old and got a speeding ticket. My dad said he was not going to pay for it so I had to find a way to make money to take care of the ticket. One of our family friends had a construction company and said I could move a mound of dirt for the money to pay the fine. He had a shovel and a wheelbarrow. That mound of dirt had sat untouched for several years. Anyway, I struggled with that dirt in the hot summer of Arkansas for what seemed like a very long time. Anyway, the end of the story I moved the dirt, got paid, paid the fine and everyone was content. It was a learning experience. It was an education. After that experience that construction company gave me a job. I will say this to the character of my dad. He didn't like the fact that I had been taken advantage of by the dirt pile owner, so in the last days of my dirt moving fiasco, my dad came to help me complete the job.

For years I pushed wheelbarrows, carried concrete, and eventually laid bricks and blocks. Sometimes I would watch others and sometimes someone would show me the tips and the tricks of the trade. This was an education. I would seek it or either it would seek me. All it cost me was my time, energy, and or effort. There was no college or university involved. I was being paid ten dollars an hour back then and that was triple what others made flipping burgers. Several years later I got a job as a painting contractor. I was an exceptional painter. I had a good eye and steady hand for cutting colors to colors. I never went to college or university to learn to paint or hold a brush, and I was making twenty dollars an hour back then and often got raises. I was making seven to eight times what the burger flippers and waitresses were making. Was I educated? You bet I was! No school or university though.

I became tired of smelling like mineral spirits and paint all the time, although I was making really good paychecks. It was time to move on and learn something new. My dad always said, "If you don't like your job find another one, try something else, it is imperative you be happy with your job". I was really good with my hands and my coordination. Since the Air Force my dad had always been involved in aircraft engineering. He bought me a drafting set. We were a middle-class family living paycheck to paycheck, so we didn't have the money to buy me a drafting table, a T-square, and all the essentials. To be able to use drafting equipment I took one single class at a vocational school in drafting.

The teacher of the class was amazed at how good I received the instruction and attained my new education in drafting and illustration. A month later I was the sole drafter within an engineering department at a local military base. I was making more at that position than my dad was making as an aerospace engineer. All I had received was one single course at a vocational school. I had plenty of motivation and all I needed was a little boost and I could figure out the rest. I didn't need a hand-out all I needed was a chance and I could make the rest happen.

I won't go into my divorce, my fall from grace, and the several years of the negativity, which brought me to the realizations of life, when I decided there must be something else in life for me. I decided that to achieve what I wanted I needed and wanted a college education. I do believe, in my situation, undoubtably, that part of that realization was I needed to be away from the negative aspects of my life. This meant moving away and at that point my best option was to move away, get student loans, and go to college. So, this is what I did. My grandmother said she would pay for my first semester, then I could get student loans, and this is what I did. I made dean's list every semester.

I decided I wanted more than this school could offer so I transferred to another school and program. I became involved in education. During my AS degree the professors would have me help the other students in the class who were not as equipped as I. The professors would single me out. I wanted to be like them. I was accepted into the BS program in career and technical education. I was also a student worker in the department all that time. The professors again prodded me. I was accepted into the MS program in career and technical education. All my professors said if you want to get into higher-level education to not stop at just an MS degree you must have a doctoral degree in that field. The rest is history. Here I am today. I didn't stop.

Does everyone need an education? Yes. Does everyone need a college or university education? No, my answer is still the same. Those same skilled jobs I had when I was young are still available today. All I needed was a little guidance, the motivation, and the desire to make money whatever amount I felt I needed. I made ten dollars an hour laying brick and block with no college or university education. I made up to twenty dollars an hour paining professionally with no college or university education. I went up to thirty dollars an hour drafting within an engineering department from taking one vocational course. One vocational course and NOT a whole two-year, four-year, five-year, seven-year or ten-year college or university program.

How about More

I do believe everyone should have access to education. I do believe everyone should have access to education if that is what they want. I do not believe that education should be free. I do believe that if you have the desire and drive to get those exceptional grades every semester you should be able to receive scholarships. I believe a student should prove themselves worthy of scholarships for the first semester, then scholarships can take over. I do think a student should prove themselves first just like I did when I started. There were no scholarships for me when I first decided to go to school. Maybe that was because I was a non-traditional student and not the typical right out of high school student. I think there is a huge waste on some students right out of high school when they really have no idea what they want to do or even if they can. They all need to have a one semester trial period before receiving any form of free ride.

Some students have no business accepting a scholarship unless they possess the necessary mental tools to handle the task of a single higher-education course let-lone a college or university program. These need to be given to students who possess those traits. Give those to the worthy and proven students.

AS to AAS Degree

I remember when I received my first college degree, an AS degree in computer electronics. The semester after I received it that university changed that degree program to an AAS. They changed an AS to an ASS degree. Downgrading for some reason. Why the downgrade? It is kind of complicated, but it does happen. I guess I will have to mention that time and the thoughts within the educational realm. I sat around with my professors, and we joked how times always evolved, revolved, and all things always changed and seemed to always come back around. Kind of like the Bell-bottom blue jeans from the 1970s, they have come back around and here we see them rampant again. Not my bag baby. Yuk.

At that time the thinking was that more of the population needed a college or university education. At that time there were vocational and technical schools everywhere, even as extensions in high schools. These were schools for skilled laborers: craftsmen, plumbers, electricians, HVAC people, masons, roofers, etc. You could even take a single course in your last year of high school, and you might get a job offer from a local construction company or affiliate. You could make a rather good living in these positions with only one single course at a vocational wing. That might be all you need to get where you want to go.

The thought, however, was let's extend the typical students' stay and keep them out of the job market for an extended amount of time and allow them the prize of a well-rounded education along with their learned tasks. In reality, at that time I was told it was to mainly keep students out of the job market longer, for either two or four years at least. Well, that is what it did. Did it help anything? Did removing some of the harder courses from the AS program help anything? Did moving to an AAS program help anything?

It pushed more students into going into college programs. When I looked at transferring, I would never have chosen an AAS program over an AS program. An AAS is more of a skilled labor program, and an AS is more of a technical program. AAS is lower level and AS is higher level. If you are involved in education, you understand the difference. As AAS is not as stringent.

The Online Travesty

In addition, at this time, there was something in the wind happening called online. My professors and I sat around and laughed. How easily that the current (brick-and-mortar) educational purview is being persuaded to move into the toilet and would at some point be flushed away. I don't know if anyone remembers. Back then, in the mid-1990s the United States Department of Education had a statement on their website that they would not get involved in accreditations, nor would they offer a listing of educational facilities on their website.

The DoE also delineated that in order for any educational facility to offer online education degrees that facility would have to have a physical residential campus. That physical residential campus was where the majority of their students would reside and complete residential programs and offering online programs would be an extension of a brick-and-mortar facility. Does anyone remember that? I do. We all sat around and joked about that too.

I remember all the ivy league schools standing up and shouting that they wanted no part of these online fly-by-night educational installations. The only true education is the physical residential education. The student gets up in the morning, goes to physical class, accesses associations with their peers, mentors, and professors, then after graduation receives recommendations from their associations and professors which ease their acceptance into the career market. Isn't this the way of the college or university education? It was back then! I physically see what you can do then I recommend you! I was back then! It was hand holding until I pass the students hand off to the employer's hand. Think: Why do you think there are so many jobs that go unfilled today? There is a reason! The reason the student does not see, will not see, and does not expect. "If you get an online education, you better already have your hand on a branch, as who is going to recommend you to employers? An online professor?" Look before you leap.

Online is fine if you are bettering yourself in the career position you already have attained. Online is not for the student who has no job or opportunity they can see prior to degree involvement. You may get the degree and fall into something by chance, but typically, it will not happen for you. Ask around and see how many out-of-work college and university graduates there are. How many received online degrees. How many didn't go into the right field or area to begin with. That is another story. My advice: If you are planning to go to any educational facility ask and research fist who hires their graduates and what is that placement percentage. You will be surprised that very few schools can offer up any such statistics. Don't fall for the "all our graduates have jobs" routine. You want to know that they have jobs in their degree area of expertise. There are little-to-no facilities that keep track of those such statistics.

Most of these facilities have alumni organizations that try to keep track of their graduates. Do they really? Are they honest? Do regulations keep them from giving you lists of their members and their career positions? Do your research. The research will not come to your door nor will the employer after you graduate. You are your guide and conductor. No matter what anyone says, you are the only true one that cares about you.

How about Now

The Ivy League schools tried to fight and lost. After several years of seeing all the money that these online schools have made, the ivy league schools finally jumped on the bandwagon to get their piece of the global online college and university pie. Go to the DoE website now and there is a section devoted to a school listing of accredited educational facilities. How times have changed. Now it seems you can have a 100% online educational facility and through holes in the system you can get accredited. All it seems to take is money. It takes money to make money.

H i g h e r E d a S c a m ?

I have been hearing a lot of this around and on certain platforms and venues. I think on one hand it might and could be and on the other hand no-so-much. Anything can be a scam if you are not researched and learned. Since the prevalent key word of today is money. Well, money could be the root of quite a few evils and often is and will always be. What is a scam exactly? A scam is said to be a dishonest scheme or fraud.

If ruling powers inform and propose every human entity within their purvey that in order to receive employment you must have a college or university education. Then that might be a fraud or scam. You can pretty much debunk that statement by doing some simple research or internet searches. Just walk down one of the streets in the business district of your town. Are there any wanted signs on the doors or windows? I would call that a scam.

There are some employment positions in the universe that require college or university degrees. Some employment positions require more than one and some require the higher levels. Some of this depends upon the positions themselves. Some employment positions require certifications. Certifications are not necessarily provided by colleges and or universities. So, therefore some employment positions may require certifications.

What I am trying to say is that it depends upon the requirements of each position. I think that is where we often get led astray in our thoughts and terminologies. I doubt I would want someone to operate on my body or inside my mind that was not an educationally trained doctor, surgeon, or therapist. I really have no need to have my new house built by a college or university degree holder.

I think part of the issue lies in the pushers or persuaders.

Of course, now that the DoE has opened the Pandora's box and allowed every mom-and-pop shop to own an online degree granting institution, here we are. All you need are some shareholders. Too many institutions that grant degrees are competing for students. There is a never-ending supply of institutions and there is a never-ending supply of potential candidates. If that supply of students does not seek you out then you must seek out those students and persuade them that you offer what they need, and what they need is necessary and required to advance and get where you want to be. Don't think for a minute that this just means within the United States, there lies a tapped and vast resource, the international student.

Post-secondary educational facilities spend large amounts of money seeking out new markets and ways to twist the data to serve their purposes. The glass can be either half-empty or half-full depending upon which side you seek. You can twist and turn data to say anything you want it to say. Data itself is stagnate and solid. Data is not flexible within itself. It is the entities that use the data for their intended purpose.

If a school says it has a 20% graduation rate. It also says it has an 80% retention rate. These are yearly terms.

Does a graduation rate mean anything? A 20% graduation rate related to what? To the student population? Depending upon how you look at it, it depends on whether it is good or bad. What about the 80% retention? 80% of what? Once again, here we go, enjoy the ride. That is 80% and how often is that calculated and against what data or facts?

Retention in the world of education is a term that relates to a student that starts in one facility and stays at that facility the whole time until their graduation. That is retention. If joe-bob starts at University X and graduates there then he has retained. Joe-bob is a retention statistic. If joe-bob leaves after his first semester, transfers, or dies, he has NOT retained. He is still a statistic. The objective is to keep a student from beginning to end, the duration of their degree seeking venture.

There are a multitude of factors that sway student retention. Maybe some or many of these factors are generational, maybe not. Maybe there are quite a few factors that depend upon the single student themselves. It seems that administration believes many of these factors are controllable, and maybe they are. Some of these just happen and that is what we call life circumstances. Some of these are student choices driven by institutions themselves. For instance: Student access too little to no extra-curricular activities for races, creeds, or orientations. Little to no cutting-edge technologies in the classrooms. I could write a book on these from what I have seen.

In fact, look at your facility. It is rather easy to review and find faults and causes. I don't think higher education is a scam, but I do think the scam is that everyone is told they need an education to be happy and make a decent amount of money. Research is the key here. Human entities get so caught up in the media hype and the mass of information present. Each human entity must do their research and make their own decisions and not rely on others to make those decisions for them. After saying that, education can be a scam if you do not do your research. You cannot put the blame on an entity that gives you an opportunity and you do not do your research, especially in this day and age of money.

Helmet Head

I think some things in life should stay the same, tradition I should say, and some things should progress. Sometimes they regress, while stumbling through progression. I doubt very few of us remember when the football helmets were nothing more than leather skullcaps. You know ones similar to those in the old war movies that pilots wore in airplanes, the ones with propellers, the fighters and bombers. There really was not much padding in those helmets in those early days. Then came progression of sorts when medical facilities started reviewing participants' head trauma and concussions. Hence, the revisions of padded helmets and later neck rolls. There has always been a battle between keeping tradition and progressing for safety. You know, you always have that faction that wants to keep it the way we always did it. The ones who often want and instigate the change are the ones negatively impacted from the old way.

I think that any sport that offers a helmet, must at some point have been researched, and the ending census reached was that a helmet should be worn for safety. It would just seem to me to be so. What other purpose would there be for the use of a helmet other than safety? Since human elements have a history of violence, I do see how sometimes those elements prefer not to use a helmet. This is prevalent in higher levels of boxing and full-contact fighting, where the basic primal premise is to knock out your opponent until he or she can take no more punishment and admits defeat. You know, the strong prevails over the weak. I do think in certain instances human elements can make the choice for themselves, the choice of whether to wear a helmet or to not. One of the most prevalent places we see options is that of motorcycle riding. I will tell you that when speaking with most motorcycle riders they will most generally say "If you ride you will eventually slide". This means that the odds are just there in play each time you get on a motorcycle. If you spend enough time on a motorcycle at some point in your future the odds are that you will in fact "slide".

I have ridden motorcycles since I was around 20 years old. I have been down on a motorcycle at over 100 miles an hour and I will never forget it. The only thing that kept me from breaking my neck was the helmet that was on my head and the back roll that supported my neck. Today I still have daily neck pain, but in all cases I cheated death. I myself will never get on a motorcycle without a helmet. Previous to this learning experience I was on a dirt bike when I was a few years younger. This is the learning experience that caused me to opt to wear the helmet in the first place. I was out on a farm riding a dirt bike. I was going through the gears when I came upon a large pile of rocks. The front wheel was on the rocks, where it somehow got caught. This all happened within a few seconds. I knew the bike was going down and out of the corner of my eye I saw a patch of tall green grass. As the bike was falling, I jumped as best I could to reach the green grass. What I did not see was the barbed wire fence separating me from the green grass. I had jumped into the barbed wire fence. I pulled a few barbs from several places in my skin. While walking away I felt something in my eye. I was wearing contact lenses in my eyes and one of the barbs had cut one of my lenses in half in my eye. That contact lens saved my eye. From that point forward, I made a pact with myself that I would always wear a helmet on a motorcycle. That is my opinion anyway.

Other than my opinion. I always thought that: What if I was in a motorcycle accident and had brain damage and could not think for myself. What if I had a passenger that had no helmet, and they got hurt because of me? Just some thoughts...I guess I do have the right to think for myself, but do I have the right to make that same decision for another?

On another note: Do we still do helmet strength testing on animals? Back when I was in my BS degree program, I wrote a paper on animal testing, specifically chimpanzees and helmet testing. They would strap a monkey into a chair, put a helmet on his head, and slam a metal rod into the helmet and see how that helmet held out during the concussion. It was quite a sinister sight. That was also during the time they were trying to well, I will not go into that as it is more disturbing.

I was watching a rodeo event the other day and now the bull riders are wearing helmets. I never thought I would see that.

Bring Out the Dead

You thought this was going to be something else didn't you. I have never understood how some populations of human entities continue to hide, overlook, and sweep under the carpet, errors and mistakes their "own kind" continue to do over and over and over time and time again. It amazes me how they continue to compound their justification and minimization. No matter the amount of money nor the negative impact or affect brought about by the culprit or culprits. Yes, it could be a single human entity or a multitude of like-minded entities.

Is this a cultural issue? Is this the past not catching up to the now? If you truly care, make an example for others to see. That example may cause the same thing from not happening again in the future. If you bury your head in the sand and the same thing happens again, whose fault is it? If that human entity uses the same plan time after time and gets away with it, they are only doing what they know works. The premise may be their fault, but after a time, whose fault is it really, when they use it time and time again? Look in the mirror. Don't put the blame on others if you looked the other way. You cannot fix the issue if you look the other way.

The Whistle-blower

Is this the last true bastion of honor and integrity? Do you realize these human entities risk all on the premise of truth. I will say that some human entities know right from wrong just as some human entities are leaders.

Some human entities throw caution in the wind and stand up for what they believe to be right. I recently went into an artificial intelligence program and asked a question about whistle-blowers. I will not copy those words here as this writing as solely my thoughts, but I will say that the answer I received from that program was 100% in favor of whistle-blowers and what they stand for and the need for them in our society.

When to say When

Do we never know when to quit? I see this quite often. This topic can relate to just about every aspect of human life on this planet, large or small. What is the stopping point when we learn a lesson? When we actually have learned that lesson. How far do we have to carry something? I try to stay out of religious issues, but we see things all the time in the news.

I remember when I was a kid and even later in my years. One thing that I always look back at and what I thought every human entity on this earth knew. That is that Israel, the small country of Israel, was always one their guard and to be left alone, as if they were bothered, they would strike back with immediate action. I thought every human entity knew that. Now, I do understand that people on this earth have peoples as enemies and some countries have enemies of other countries.

Currently, in this world there are wars going on between nations. Here we are again, that another country is pushing Israel. Air strikes between two factions. These two countries have been rivals for a long time. They are once again, playing the "I got you last" card. Massive loss of civilian life on both sides. I guess that is one of the things I don't really get about some of these wars, is when civilian lives are lost. But I guess the war has to be carried out somewhere other than on a chess board. It has to happen somewhere.

I also do understand that religion has brought forth more loss of life than any pestilence or combination of suffering than anything else on this planet. Do we not have religious freedom? I always thought we did. Why must I push my religious belief down the throat of another human entity? I have the freedom to pursue others to bring them to my visions, but in a peaceful manner. I have always thought that anyway.

Now, I do think we understand that wars are started and governed by the higher powers and entities that be. It isn't the lower classes and the supposed nobodies of the time that cause these issues, it is the rulers and guiders of those nations. We will always have and there will always be leaders and followers.

I guess part of my answer to this topic is the culture of each nation on this earth. It is all in the teaching and learning from the day we are born. It all stems from the training we receive from the people and relationships around us. I think the main driver of this may also be the religious writings and teachings that we receive. Some books teach forgiveness and others teach persuasion.

I am not a biblical scholar by any means, but I do have some scriptures that stick in my mind for one reason or another.

"Father, forgive them; for they do not know what they are doing".

"Blessed are the peacemakers, for they shall be called sons of God".

"Let us therefore make every effort to do what leads to peace…"

"Follow peace with all men…"

Infest or Invest

Do we understand the difference between infestation and investation? I know, I'm not here to put a new word in the dictionary. Anyway. I think by now we all understand the premise of the strong will overcome the weak. If we look at the history of quite a few countries we can see where this applies or has applied. The United States was infested by any other population other than what was currently here at the time. Typical of a lot of places on maps. That generally is what happens when you put a destination on a map. Human entities see that map and their curiosity peaks and their inhibitions subside, and they are off into the sunset to see it for themselves.

At first it is an infestation, then later comes the investation. Infesting is like a bug that is introduced into a situation and takes advantage of that situation and survives. Investing is when that same bug over time advances from that advantage situation and survives through some sort of symbiotic situation or situations with other bugs or entities. At first you take siege of an opportunity then after that conquering, you sit back and see how best to survive through benefit offerings and transitions with other entities or populations. Share the wealth, I guess you could say.

Take for instance: The apocalypse comes, and human entities are trying to survive. Some entities have prepared for the coming of this and many more have not. The struggle is upon us. You go from clique to clique looking for a safe haven for you and your family. You knock on the door, the door opens, and you are asked what you can provide for the community. What can you do or what can you offer to help others sustain their existence? If you cannot provide anything you may be turned away. This would/could be a symbiotic relationship. Maybe you have no skill at the time, and you are offered to be taught a skill? Everyone can provide something, I would think.

Even the strumming of a lute could help others at naptime or bedtime. That could be a skill. It might seem trivial at this time but let's cross that bridge when we come to it. That would be a symbiotic relationship.

Our US History

I think most human entities reading this writing know of the history of this country, the United States. Some big-name dude from some other country was out floating around the oceans, saw some land and declared ownership by his country by sticking a flag in the soil, yada, yada, yada. Then other human entities got curious and came and came and came. Here we are today. I would guess at this moment in time symbiotic relationships abound. Human entities working together for the common good. Isn't the common good what most of us are trying to achieve?

O p - E d

Me being born in the United States and living here for my years from what I can see there are a few things that are truly on the top of the list if you want to live in this country. Now, there are the ten commandments brought down by Moses but those are not the ones I am speaking of, that is another story.

The ones I am speaking about are: Pay your taxes and stay out of trouble. Yes, there are addendums and add-ons, but these are the most prevalent and the base of any others that may come into play. Now is that so hard? Pay your taxes and stay out of trouble.

I cannot say that these are easy tasks. Life isn't simple and easy. Sometimes we try to make it that way but it sems there is always something standing in the path, some obstacles to overcome, to achieve what we think we need or want to achieve. Sometimes that or those may not be in our best interest, but we try them anyway. I guess that mixes with the stay out of trouble part we often see to have little to no control over.

If you have a role to play do your part. Don't push your part off to someone else. If you must pay taxes to reside, then pay your taxes. I am like a lot of other human entities that complain about things we see. Every time I am driving along, and my tire drops into a hole or crater in the road and it about jars the teeth out of my head I complain. "I pay my taxes, what does this state do with my tax money, fix this damn hole!" It seems like every week something crosses my lips. Anyway, I guess tax money only goes so far. I guess you cannot fix every single issue that comes to life.

All the government wants is its cut of your proceeds. The government wants its population to be productive. All it wants is its cut of the proceeds of your success. Pay the man. That is all you have to do to keep the man happy and fulfill my first rule: Pay your taxes. I think the Bible even has a quote: "Pay Caesar's things to Caesar". Something like that.

Do Your Part

Human entities are bad about procrastination. Putting things off until tomorrow when we know we need to do them today. Well, I was going to pay taxes, I forgot, something else came up. Have you ever heard or said these before. Some people say them and most get caught and put on the spot, when they least expect it. If you know you need to do it, you better make a point to handle it, then all will be well in your world. If you put it off, you take a chance.

I do not know why it takes so long to achieve citizen status in the United States or any other country for that matter. Why does it take so long? All the country wants is your tax dollars going into their system. They want you to be a paying citizen just like the rest. They want you to take your part in handling the burden. You have to pay for your piece of the pie. At least, in my opinion, that is what I think they want. It seems to work for all the citizens I know.

It just seems like you come to the USA for a better life. Invest your money in the USA and not the other country you say you are trying to escape from. You come to the USA and send money home to your friends and family is not what the government wants, so you are not paying your part as they see it. All they want is what they feel is their due. Don't give anyone any reason to come looking for you. Don't put a target on your back if and when you can avoid it.

Two Schools

As far as my personal experience, I have seen two schools of thought in relation to post-secondary institutions. I will label them here as "Transparent U" and "Beard U". First, let me explain what I mean by the titles of these schools as they are run by two completely different administrations. The dictionary defines transparent as allowing light to pass through so that objects can be seen and or have thoughts, feelings, or motives that are easily perceived. The normal definition for beard refers to the hair growth on a man's cheeks or chin. Apparently, this definition is not what I am looking for so I will go with the slang definition, which refers to describe any situation where someone is used as a façade to hide a different reality, either intentionally or unintentionally. Now that makes more sense and fits this topic.

I draw a simulation between these two entities as street musicians in the subway or on the corner. There are two musicians, one on the corner of the street across from each other. The one on the first corner is known as: "Transparent U". This is a person with a big smile on their face picking away on the banjo. As people walk by, they stop, sing along, and tap their feet. At the foot of the musician there is a hat overflowing with dollars left by the happy patrons. This musician has learned he/she must produce a quality product to get paid. This is a symbiotic relationship of sorts. This is what every post-secondary institution strives to achieve.

The second musician on the other corner is known as: "Beard U". This proposed musician is sitting in a chair watching the passersby with a concerned look on his/her face. He/she is wondering why the others are passing by, walking to the other corner, stopping for a time, then handing over dollars to that musician. This entity is constantly looking at the empty hat at their feet and wondering what the problem is. All the potential patrons, the passersby, see and realize the issue but the musician does not seem to understand. The musician thinks they know something all the potential patrons do not, but alas that is wrong thinking, as the patrons realize to earn money you need to produce a quality product. You only get paid when you produce. No one gets paid before they see what product is developed. They need to see if that product fits their needs.

Now let's delve into the world of both these quite different universities and the perceived mentality behind those walls.

Transparent U

This is what the typical layman might consider the majority of the post-secondary educational facilities. These are the ones that closely work with the communities around them. They always seem to give access to the communities, and the communities always seem to involve them in everything revolving around them. It is a true symbiotic relationship. You never see one entity without involving the other. A true handholding symbiotic relationship.

It is true that these institutions of learning are sometimes plagued with bad apples, the bad leadership that sometimes makes the headlines. Majority of the time these institutions bring forth the culprit and make an example out of him/her. The point here is that an example is made from that issue. By making that example, it says to the next administrator applying to that facility that form of behavior will be challenged, not allowed to fester, and removed like a cancerous cell. This is a critical step in the running of a facility of this nature.

This facility is driven and ran by a cabinet of administrators, each having responsibilities. This facility is run by what we call a system of checks and balances. This system is made to hopefully keep things within the university upright and honest. It would be wrong of me to say these facilities are perfect. They are not perfect, as they are only as perfect as non-perfect humans can be under this form of regime that has enabled checks and balances. Some of these institutions or their leaders fall from grace but it isn't often and expected. The employees at this university know what to expect, generally are content, understanding of rules, regulations, policies, and expectations, and for the most part know where they stand.

Beard U

This educational facility is a stark contrast to the one previously mentioned. The leaders of this facility do not understand how to pilot a garbage scow out of New York harbor, let alone a multi-million-dollar post-secondary educational facility. These institutions are plagued with lawsuits and whistleblowers. Honesty in fact does seem to go unrewarded. These institutions have top level administrators that micro-manage the experienced personnel. They micro-manage as they think they have an answer that no one else knows or sees. This is often not true. It is the long-term personnel who have the answers, but no one ever looks to them for the answers that could so easily be explained. This facility has no checks and balances. Anyone finding discrepancies is most often terminated for their findings resulting in more lawsuits.

At these facilities, you will generally see high spending at the top tiers of administration, most often padding their resumes and bank accounts with facility monies. A school may be in trouble financially, but that does not stop the excessive amount of expenses from new administrations. These facilities say they want to be part of the communities around them, but in fact they do not want to give any outside entities any kudos for helping or assisting in any endeavors. They want to say they are self-made with no outside interference. They fail to give credit where credit is due. If you are not in the clique, you are never acknowledged for your participation.

These are the facilities that we want to stay in the past. They do not want any outside interference, even if it is positive.

You know there are problems when you have meetings and are told to keep all the information in-house. Any time someone spouts the term in-house you understand there are negative issues abounding. Who is trying to hide what from who?

One-Third Control

I guess we all understand that we are all products of our environments, the good, the bad, and the ugly. We also understand that there is no such thing as a self-made human entity. A self-made human entity would throw the "product of our environment" theory out the window.

My whole existence, or at least my existence when I started to get a little educated, I have always said that we, human elements, have been our own guide and conductors through the traveled path called life. Maybe that thinking is not as I once thought. It finally dawns on me that as far as a human element: a human's existence is split into three. Three of what? Three pathways, scenarios, or what? I cannot really pinpoint what these might be called. I find that there are three factors that play out in each human life no matter where you come from, how much money you have, etc. Those would be a human entity committing suicide or by their own hand, a human entity becoming the victim of homicide or at the hand of another form or entity, and the final one natural causes. Given each of these, 33.333 percent for each of three, this mere calculation blows the theory that each of us are our own guides and conductors. This tells us that we are only a third responsible for our lives and outcomes and the other two-thirds are provided by other means.

So, then I guess we bring into question each of those thirds. Is there a numerical scale or limitation we can truly see for each human element to control that one third they truly control? Does that one third have a scale of 1 to 10 or 1 to 100? How do we know when we achieve all we can or want to achieve? How do we know when we have made it?

I know it can get complicated. I think life can become quite complex. I just thought I would throw in something more to think about.

Why so Complicated

Why does life seem to be so complicated? We are born; we live then we pass on. A revolving door we someday can get leave. It revolves day in and day out. Round and round.

Does life have to be complicated? Do we just make it that way? They always say, "Work smarter not harder". Are there many times where we look back and see we did not work smarter? I would guess so. It seems that every day we encounter things we may not have seen before, so that makes all of those times learning experiences. Currently, I am up to about learning experience 6,924, and it still keeps climbing.

It seems the less people I know and come into contact with the less complicated life seems. Does it just seem to be this way? If I have 100 Facebook friends or 10,000, does it make a difference in my life complications? Maybe that is a little drastic or not a good relationship as I can delete any and all of them anytime, I want, and those human entities have no real bearing on my existence unless I care what each of them think about me or me them. I guess that is where the complication comes into play. Typically, there are human entities in each of the lives of each human entity that may care about what they think, say and do. It seems the more human entities we know the more complicated our lives become if we care about the way they view us and the way we view them.

C o n j u n c t i o n   J u n c t i o n

The title of this topic might not really fit. Why did I pick it. When I was a kid sitting in front of the TV on Saturday morning there were quite a few commercials and things that were made to hopefully educate whoever was watching. One of the tidbits that came had a catchy tune that still pops into my head today. "Conjunction junction what's your function?" was one of those. It was one of many. Another one was "I'm just a Bill." Then there was one I vaguely remember about a wagon train and a piece of cheese put onto a round cracker than rolled away "Look, a wagon wheel." These may not mean anything to you but to me, they are priceless memories. All of them tried to teach us something between cartoons. Try and find and see something like this today.

There are three branches in the United States Federal government. They are the executive, legislative, and judicial.

The executive branch is led by the President and Vice President. This branch enforces the laws of the nation. The Vice President oversees over what is called the Senate. Under the President there is a group of individuals called a cabinet. This cabinet is comprised of "smart people" who are specialists in their areas of expertise. For instance: If you are the President and you have no background in military matter you would have a cabinet member who has expertise in that are that you could ask advice from if you were so inclined.

The legislative branch is comprised of a group of people called congress. This congress is made up of what we call congress men and women and there are 100 members. These congress men and woman are also called senators. In addition to these senators there is a group of 435 members called a House of

Representatives. There are 435 representatives. These two bodies or groups of people are the ones who make the laws that the executive branch enforces. Each senator will serve a six-year term, and each representative will serve a two-year term. These people are elected by the people and can serve more than one term. Each state in the United States has two senators and each state has a delegated number of representatives dependent upon the size of that state's population.

The judicial branch interprets the laws made by the legislative branch that are enforced by the executive branch. This branch can come between the legislative and executive branch when new laws are to be considered or made and this branch can also be brought into play after laws have been made to interpret the true meaning of them after the fact. Governing this branch is what we have called a supreme court. This is the highest level of court within the United States. This supreme court is made up of nine members called justices.

These three branches have what are called checks and balances. These are put into play to ensure that no one branch has more power than the other branch. I guess we could say that each branch has one-third of the total power. No one branch is over any other branch or branches.

We hear all the time that the President of the United States is nothing more than the face of a nation. I like to think it is more than just that. I think there is a lot of responsibility that comes with that office and other subordinate offices under that title.

Yes, the President can sign an executive order. An executive order is an order given by the President delineating some action to be taken. Some action to be taken by the executive branch. If you remember earlier, I was talking about the branches. This executive order may be reviewed before or after the fact of it being given to make sure that order does not override existing laws or the constitution in which governs the United States. If it has been found that it does, then it can be stopped or rescinded.

The President may be the face or a nation. He may be able to push executive orders, but the checks and balances of each branch can put a halt if it is found unconstitutional or impeding or infringing upon any existing law. The President can bring forth and ideas or concepts felt wanted or needed, but the senators and representatives must be on-board and approve those ideas and or concepts to take place. The President may be the face we see, and he or she may be the one we hold accountable or responsible but in fact the senators and representatives are the true ones that are held accountable. It is easier to blame one single person other than the majority of a political party when things go bad.

T o o   M a n y   P e o p l e

I was asked by students in class why so many people were having babies. This led to a conversation more related to the fact that people are now living longer than they ever have on this planet. The Covid virus had massively exterminated over one million human entities within the United States. If we look previous to my first birthday in the 1960s, we will find that many of the diseases and pestilences from those years are not so applicable today. The wars we have today do not have the death tolls that were prevalent at those times. I am really only speaking of the United States, as other countries do have some or most of the same conditions they have had for long periods of time. If I go back to the original thought from the student asking about babies, it always boggles me when a population is starving, and they continue to make babies.

It is like, "I don't have a job to go to, so hey, how about since we are home anyway, let's make another baby". I never have been able to comprehend that.

Literate Illiterate

I hear a lot of administrators talk about competency-based education. I think they get confused as they have nothing more than artificial intelligence knowledge of this phenom. It seems when you hear them talk with the big words, you quickly realize they have never read a physical book on that specific topic, then they think and portray themselves as the all-knowing entity. It becomes quite comical. "Read a book for once, the whole book, not just the first, middle, and last pages".

I call it puzzle-based education. My question is: How can you work a puzzle if you have no knowledge of what the puzzle should look like when completed. It is like putting together pieces of a puzzle with no face. One hundred pieces of strange, shaped pieces and no picture on the box of what the finished outcome should look like. That is the problem. Or you have a picture of the finished product and no instructions on how to get there.

How about an example: I teach a course called X. We will learn about X. We will learn the beginnings and current uses of X. This will generally take, as in all topics, an understanding that we need to memorize and practice all things related to X. We want to have a grounding and base of knowledge of X. Right? If I give students a brief synopsis about X and then give them puzzles related to X. Students may be able to pass the puzzles of X, but what about all the underlying information we bypass relative to X? When they pass the class of X can they talk the talk and walk the walk as it relates to X? What you basically would be doing is breezing through the topic of X, and passing on the student who has little-to-no real knowledge of X. You have plenty of students who pass with passing grades but no real knowledge of X.

Why would a learning facility want to move to this form of learning? Does that facility accept students who are vastly unprepared? Does that facility have an issue with student retention? Why would a facility move to this type of strategy? Are there other simpler ways to meet the issues other than re-tooling existing practices? This is one of those things where faculty need to be consulted, as they are the ones physically on the ground with the student population. If you lower the standards by which the majority of corporate owners and leaders went through in their educational attainment, will those leaders opt-out of hiring, when they realize what was good for them is not the same as what is prevalent in an employee? So, with these graduates do we have a literate illiterate graduate? Do the math.

Simple Mathematics

I have recently been involved in a discussion of mathematics courses viable in university education. The two culprit courses under review are college algebra and contemporary mathematics. Some major degree programs need only contemporary mathematics as a general education requirement and other more stringent programs (engineering and the sciences) need college algebra and sometimes higher-level math courses after.

The question is: Does an educational facility have the right to make all students, regardless of their major, take college algebra when most facilities in the United States only make their students take contemporary mathematics? It seems like a simple choice, if you are a mathematician, but not so simple if you struggle with abstract math. Contemporary math is most certainly easier to pass for the typical unprepared student, rather than the more stressful algebra. This isn't the less high-school algebra, this is the more college algebra. Math professors abound to make the argument that administration has no right to make students take the higher level of math over the lower level of math. When a parent of student asks if they must take college algebra or the lower-level contemporary, who will lie to them? Who will give them the reasoning?

A D i s s e r v i c e

It can be a disservice to require students to take college algebra when contemporary math would better align with their needs, goals, and academic pathways. Contemporary math often covers practical, real-world applications (like financial literacy, statistics, logic, or voting systems), which are more relevant than the abstract algebraic concepts in college algebra.

College algebra can become an unnecessary source of student anxiety and a formidable barrier or roadblock for capable students whose strengths lie outside STEM. If a general education math course is meant to promote Quantitative literacy, Critical thinking. And Real-world problem-solving contemporary math would fulfil their needs better than college algebra for non-STEM students. Colleges need to follow the Math Pathways movement, which advocates aligning math courses to students' programs of study. For example: STEM → Calculus path, Social Sciences → Statistics, and Liberal Arts → Contemporary Math.

Making students take college algebra unnecessarily risks harming motivation, delaying progress, and failing to equip them with relevant skills. Math education should serve the student's goals, not hinder them. The key here would be to: advise students of their options instead of just enrolling them into a course. Requiring algebra for all students can misrepresent what "being good at math" really means. Contemporary math may be more meaningful, practical, and inclusive for most students, which will better prepare them for everyday life, not just academia.

In Comparison

Algebra requires abstract reasoning: working with variables, symbolic manipulation, and generalized rules. Struggle with algebra is not a sign of low intelligence; it often reflects gaps in prior instruction, math anxiety, or misalignment with personal strengths. In fact, national and global data consistently show that algebra is a major stumbling block for college students.

Contemporary math focuses on real-life, applicable concepts like basic statistics, personal finance, probability, logical reasoning, and mathematical modeling. These skills are universally useful in voting, budgeting, interpreting data, or making informed decisions. It's often more engaging and intuitive for students outside of technical fields.

It is one-thing to challenge the honor and integrity of an educator, but it is quite another to ask them to lie for something they know is highly questionable in the least. Why should a student have to struggle and possibly fail college algebra multiple times when they only need to pass contemporary mathematics which is more useful in the world around them? How many times can a student fail a course? How many times should a student fail a course until you just pass them, to let them proceed? Does this also affect/effect student retention, which is a topic in this day and time?

Book Smart

Are you just book smart and little else? Do you just have one topic that you know inside and out? Growing up I was always told that educators knew their topic only and little else.

For instance: I was always told that if you were an English teacher that you probably knew everything there was to know about English and little else. It was also mentioned in the same breath "Those who can do, and those who can't, teach". This is questionable. I see both sides. Now we have another premise to add to this idea, AI smart. First, we had street smart, then at the same time we had book smart, now we have to add AI smart. At some point in our human past street smart was considered common sense, but that has long since passed. Common sense is some whimsical idea that came from the dark side of the moon, or at least maybe that is where it spends its days now.

Book smart cannot make you street smart. Street smart cannot make you book smart. AI smart cannot make you either and neither can make you AI smart. It's complicated. We just make it that way.

Convert or Slain

Why do religions think they have to concert everyone? Why do human entities think they have the right to slaughter populations of what they call infidels? The infidels that do not succumb to their way of thinking. Anyone who studies human history knows that religion or the thought of religion has killed more people in the name of religion than any combination of pestilence, plague, or epidemic since the beginning of time, that we are aware.

Remember the crusades? Remember the Holocaust? Remember the inquisition? Religion was the prime driver. If you go to a homeless shelter or a place to eat if you have no money and are maybe starving, do they make you listen to a sermon first? Is there some stipulation to receive what is being provided? Why does everything have stipulations or processes of hoops to partake? Why do we make things so complicated?

I remember quite a few years back there were missionaries called "end-of-timers". These missionaries would go to foreign countries and spread their religious words. Part of their spreading the word was to initiate the people into bringing the apocalypse (end-of-times) in as short of time as can be. Helping bring forth the apocalypse as swiftly as possible. Assisting it in coming. I guess the thinking was "why wait, when we can help it along". Isn't that like taking it out of God's hands when you profess to be a follower of God? That just didn't seem to make sense to me. Maybe they just professed and were actually wolves in sheep clothing?

What is the saying "Beware of Greeks bearing gifts". That really does not apply here as this saying is related to the Trojans and the Greeks when they were warring nations. You know the story, the wooden horse, yada, yada, yada. They were enemies not missionaries supposedly coming to help a population of people. How can you claim to help a people when you push them to the deadly brink of a possible no return?

W a r

As with most family trees, there is a lot of military involvement in mine. First, I will say there is nothing good about war. Sometimes good may come from war, but during those durations' bleakness pervades. Just to name a few positive outcomes. My great grandfather was the sixth man to receive the CMH from his exploits during the Civil War in this United States of America. My dad's brother was a member of the Office of Strategic Services (OSS) during World War II (WWII). He was a spy and was captured by the Japanese and put into a prison camp. One day toward the end of the war the Japanese ordered all the prisoners out of their huts and lined up into rows. The Japanese officers were beheading the prisoners one at a time. One prisoner from my uncle was next in line when allied tanks crashed through the gates liberating the camp. These were positive outcomes.

This topic isn't about my family history it is about war and some of the things we take for granted. Some of the realizations some civilians do not understand and most certainly never will. Unless you have been in the mud, been in the suck, been in the "Whatever you want to call it), you have little to no idea of the reality those human elements face before, during, and or after".

I believe we are products of our environment from the day we are born and arrive into this world with open eyes and ears. Listening and seeing everything we can, positive and negative. That makes us who we are. Simply spending a little time to read what I have written here makes you different than you were before reading it.

Think of the typical age of the human element recruited or drafted during war time. It is hard to believe that sometimes they could be as young as 15 or 16 years of age. We don't see that much anymore but look at history. Even at 17 or 18 years of age, is that much different than 15 or 16? Think about it. Think back when you were 15 to 18, would you have been prepared for war or were you prepared for war? At that span of ages, or even a few years past those, would you or could you have been prepared to serve? Think of where you were at that time in your lives and what thoughts were going through your minds.

Here comes my topic point. You are taken or voluntarily removed from the short span of life you know and put into a grinder of the like you have never seen, felt, or experienced before. You stand in line to get a shaved head, you stand in line to turn your head and cough, you stand in line to get a shower, you stand in line to get screamed at by a man in a hard, brown-brimmed hat jamming your forehead and shouting at what seems to be your nose. I dare you smile! He is not looking for friends, he is not making them either! You believe him to be your worst nightmare, but he is preparing you to live or die! In a stretch of the imagination, he is your best friend and the all-knowing mentor for your survival! Skip to the fields of battle.

Sometimes there are plans of time spent in preparation but sometimes escalations happen and those plans become shortened. The proverbial bootcamp can become a shortened exam-cram. We have always heard the United States has the best prepared military. I really doubt anyone will get on television and say we are not.

There you are thrown to the wolves, relying on whatever past experiences will guide you through. Now you are to carry out any order given to you by a superior or face the consequences. Sometimes you may even face the consequences of carrying out those orders. It seems like everything in life has some kind of consequence proposed or given by someone else. Some other human entity, generally one that has no idea of the attached realities pre or post imposed.

Some human entities are frailer, and some are tougher than others. Some have entertained street-smarts, and some haven't. In most cases you can thank the poorer class populations for providing the supplied mass body count. In few cases you might say the collegiate or educated officers, the proverbial coms (commissioned) and or the non-coms (non-commissioned).

Think of the human minds molded and shaped before, during and after wartime. Think of all those experiences intertwined within the human brain. Think of the mass of thoughts. Now that you have been turned on and the hostilities have ended, how do you turn the valve off? It isn't simply a switch, contrary to popular belief. I guess that is why the civilian population has little to no idea of the issues related to these returning populations. Think of the numbers of the population of the United States. Think of the numbers of the population of military entities within the population of the United States. The military is what, maybe around one half of a percent of the total population, if even that?

If you think about those numbers. If you were building a car that you wanted to sell, to make a profit, would you build a car to meet the needs of less than one percent of the population of customers or the other ninety-nine percent? I think we know the answer here. The resources and support, which are typically in monetary form, follow the larger customer base and not the miniscule veteran population. I guess you can also chalk that up to the largest voting population too. Hence why is there a small population that does anything for the homeless or the veteran population. Just the facts.

These human entities are released from war and come back home to what they vaguely remember. If you want an example, think back to when you were a kid. Can you remember a food that you really liked at the time. Remember how great it tasted, and you always wanted to find it again and relive those past mouth-watering experiences. Oh my, I finally found that food from my past and I can't wait to try it again. Then the time comes, you take a bite! Yuk, that was not what I remember! Things seem to have changed and yes, they are different. I have done that too, and someone or something decided that item from my past needed to be improved. You try to control the on/off switch you think exists. Majority of the time, you cannot reach or find the proverbial switch. Things just seem to not make sense, at least the sense you thought once existed in your mind at a previous place and time.

I seem to be getting off topic. In the US we have a growing population of homeless and many of those homeless suffer from issues. Many of the issues are the reason they have become homeless in the first place.

I'm not homeless but I have an example of priorities. Priorities give us the base for our existence. Those priorities keep us in check. That checklist of priorities delineates the bane of our existence and how that existence relates to each other. About two years ago I incurred an issue within my internal organs. I have no idea where it came from, how it started, and doctors didn't know either and still don't. The internal pain was unbelievable. Suicide was a daily thought. My two dogs would stare at me with their tails wagging while I was sitting and crying at the horrendous pain. My Ruger 45 was always within reach. Just when I come to the point of decision I would think about my two dogs. How could they survive without me or me without them! That was the sole reason for my surviving.

The daily pain was so intense the priorities in my life changed. If I got mail it was briefly gone through and discarded. The mail wasn't more important than the pain I assure you. Anyway, a year and a half later I accidentally found a doctor, he treated my issue, and I became a new man at that point! Prior to the final doctor and end to my pain during that time span of pain

I did not respond to demands from my insurance company to pay my premiums. This ended up being a lapse in my vehicle coverage. They didn't care about my plight or any reasoning I had for missing any payments, so they doubled the amount of my premiums because I let the policy lapse. Why did the policy lapse? Because I had to change my priorities to survive the pain at that time.

Think about the priority changes that probably occurred to put human entities on the street. Put on the shoes of a veteran, if you have never worn those shoes.

Living in Fear

There have been recent issues abounding. A political pundit was recently assassinated on a university campus, Charlie Kirk. Something twenty years ago you would have never thought could happen. That idea would never have entered your thought process at that time. The next few days what a media frenzy. Like sharks in the water after your wife is missing her roast from the freezer. Everyone has an opinion. Even I have an opinion. My opinion is that: That assassination could have been prevented and should have never happened. There should have been something called security at that event. There should have been a counter-sniper above where Charlie was sitting to seek out and dismiss and sniper within his purvey. This counter-sniper would have ceased that assassination attempt in the bud.

After this assassination political pundits from both sides of the aisle condemn the action. Pundits are saying how they get death threats all the time and they will not live in fear of those threatening them. Some say they have had millions of threats over the years.

Here is my reason for this topic: In my opinion living in fear is when you live in a basement with no windows and you never leave for a fear that something might happen to you. There are different names for different types of fears that you have. I don't know of a name given to the fear of being assassinated by another human element. Maybe there is one? I'm just not a scholar of that topic.

It is one thing to live in fear as I have stated and to live in the fear of something happening and you taking extra precautions to keep that fear from becoming a reality for you, yourself, or your family. That is another type of fear. I guess the real problem is the idea or ideal generated by the mind of the human element that "it isn't going to happen to me". Well, in reality it isn't going to happen to you until it does. Then when it does happen to you, then you may not have hindsight to fix something as you may have had your existence terminated. You do not have to live in fear you just have to take extra precautions to keep your fears from occurring. That really is all you can do anyway.

Quite a few times in my past people have mentioned "Gods will". They say that if it is Gods will for their life to end than that is his will and it cannot be changed. Do you mind if I pick that apart?

I am not a biblical scholar by any means, but I did grow up around and inside a Christian religion. There are quite a few things in the lives of a human element that are under the responsibility of the human element. For the human element to just throw all their inhibitions in the air and jump off of a bridge into speeding traffic and say if I live or die it is Gods will, I see that as ludicrous and irresponsible. That is like sewing a steak onto your shirt and getting into a cage with a bear and saying well, if its Gods will. You might not like that answer as you are trying to get out of the cage. Then you want to have the bear shot for what comes to him naturally. "Thanks for the steak and dissert you moron" says the bear as he/she licks his/her chops.

Sometimes we just need to sit back and think and not tempt fate.

Conspiracy

How many people in the world disappear without a trace or under some strange circumstance? Do you know of anyone? I have known quite a few from my past. Do you ever mean keeping in touch with someone and never really seem to have the time? Do years go by and you mean well, but you know how life just seems to pass on by. This could even be family members. Have you ever went a pretty large span of time and not really had the time to physically go to where they live and actually shake their hand? You talk to them over the internet or over the telephone and all seems to be well. Are they really where you think they are? Could they really be somewhere else? Think of how long technologies have been around. Could the wool be pulled over your eyes? You think you know something as a fact, but do you really?

Something is only a conspiracy if it isn't actually and realistically happening. It is a conspiracy if there is no fact to back it up, if it is pure conjecture. Or little facts for that matter.

I have known many military people who were specialists in their fields of expertise that have died under strange circumstances. Part of those strange circumstances is that no physical body was ever found, or has been found since, they just seemed to have went away and been parched from the map. I really do not think most people quite grasp the reality of this happening or the possible necessity of this occurrence. Some human entities are just so good at what they do and cannot easily be replaced or trained in a short amount of time. That is just the reality. From past experience I truly believe this happens and is unquestionable. I will not go into detail and throw out names as I would never want to compromise anyone who might be participating in covert activity to assist my country. I'll just leave this topic at that.

On a similar note, I have had law enforcement friends run background checks on human elements in the past. They came back and said that person must have been involved in some things in their past as that person had apparently spent a lot of money having his life cleansed from the internet. They generally only see that as a red flag when someone is so clean. I would agree with that, after dealing with some of those beings.

Climate Change

Has every previous population on this planet worried about climate change? Have they experienced some form or type of change? Is this just something we see happening during our time? Did the human element cause this or is this just something that naturally occurs and is expected?

I guess there are two elements that drive this thing we humans call knowledge, religion and science. Does religion make sense and has an answer or does science make sense and has an answer? They both seem to butt heads quite a bit. Since there is no human on this planet that was actually around during the time of either, then are they not both a belief and speculation?

Religious people say that religion has the answers and scientific people say that science has the answers. I have never known any that say you can combine the two. If we look at science isn't that always changing? Don't scientists come up with new things all the time related to science? Isn't that the same with religious scholars, and they call it new light? Who can be believed when it all conjecture and a belief.

It is like politics, what side you believe is the side you want to believe in or possibly the side that makes the most sense when given the facts. What are the facts? Are they the facts that were just revealed? Where are the artifacts of those facts? Science seems to be never ending, and I guess as far as that goes religion too. They have no end. The logic of the human brain continuously seeks answers.

Look at all the previous populations that have been on this planet. All of them have died out for one reason or another, so we are told. That is what is written in our history books. Look at all the previous cities, cultures, etc. They have all been destroyed. That is what our history books tell us. Was climate change responsible for any of this? Were there sooth-sayers and philosophers that looked and kept track of climate changes and issues? Were there human elements that warned the populations of changes and devastation?

It is often said that science can only do so much and there are a lot of things it cannot explain. Isn't that the reality of virtually everything? There is no end to knowledge, there is no end to updating that current knowledge with improved knowledge. There are often brick walls to explanations but, are not those obstacles generally overcome with advances in technologies? From what I see the answer is yes, the human element is ever evolving. I'm not talking about man evolving from apes, I am speaking of man and its daily evolution of life. Everything evolves or maybe I should use the term adapt. Everything adapts, or does everything adapt? Maybe some things don't adapt then they die out. What about extinction? Why have things become extinct? Is extinction a natural occurrence of things, the dying out of the weaker element? Maybe I have asked more questions that I have answered here?

Are human elements responsible for climate change or is it a natural occurrence? If we are responsible, is it too late to stop it? Is our current civilization just another that will have an end either by our own hand or the hand of nature? Maybe our current civilization is just another Rome or ancient Greece? Was the flood of Noah's time a natural act? If you believe…

Raise the Dead

We are all just human beings. We all just want to live and pursue happiness. The older I get the more I come into contact with death. I don't like it, but it is a fact of life, that thing called death. There are many people we come into contact with during our time on this planet. One thing I really don't get is that some human entities want to keep kicking the dead horse. A person dies and you think you have some sort of right to keep pestering and pestering and pestering. Do you think you are going to sway some sort of legacy that person had? That person is dead. How about a simple "Rest in Peace" …That person has passed from this earth or whatever you believe. Do you really think you need to keep gigging, gigging, and gigging. That human entity is far past caring about what you have to say about them. Can we just be the better person and just forgive and live and let live.

Who Cares

I have a bone to pick with automakers. You should have the same bones too. Do any of them really care about the customers other than just spouting out in the media that they do?

My first bone. We are told not to take our eyes off the road. If that is the case: Why does the computer screen on my new vehicle tell me not to take my eyes of the road but has me take them off the road to push the button while I am driving to see the screen?

My second bone. This has been an on-going issue with many years and quite a few lives lost. My first bone probably has some of those too. Anyway, do you remember the days before electric door locks and windows. Windows had this roll up knob to move the windows up and down. Each one of them had one. What happens if a driver is in a vehicle and it goes off the road or a bridge into the water? One thing that happens is the electricity shorts out and does not work. The second thing is a vehicle is not really air-tight and even if it was the deeper the vehicle goes into the water the more pressurized the interior gets. There is no way you are going to have enough strength in your fist to bust out safety glass. You better be quick to think as you are heading toward the water to roll down your windows. That is a stretch but think before you drown.

When is Enough, Enough

I see and hear a lot of people in the spotlight doing just the most unreal or unbelievable things. What is up with that? When you have a celebrity that pretty much owns a large piece of the world and can almost realistically buy anyone or anything their heart desires, where do they draw the line or reality? Do they really feel they are above all laws, rules, and regulations? Do they honestly believe that? Is there ever a switch in their brain that tells them when to time out?

When do they say when? Is the sky the limit? Has there been no one or nothing in their lives that keeps them grounded in reality? Maybe they are so used to having piles of money and no limits that the only thing that makes them realize something is taking away some of those piles of money. I guess it is like having a bully. When that bully has dominance over the human entities that surround them, I guess, is part of the problem. No one wants to lose their job, right, so no one ever says anything. No one ever brings forth questions as long as they are getting paid. Then when questions arise, who jumps from the sinking ship and has an opinion. Maybe this leads back to one of my previous topics: friends. Maybe they really just never had any. Maybe they just alienated everyone around them, maybe it truly is their fault for being that way? Did the human population make them that way or did they make themselves that way?

What Age is Regression

I think one of the things that really try my patience are when other adults do child-like things. Things that make you think they think you are a child. You don't get to be my age and have achieved the things I have by having the mind, mental capacity, or the drive or strive of a child. When you treat me as if I am a child, I have a real problem with that.

I have mentioned before, "Are you trying to make me believe that, or are you trying to make yourself believe that?"

For instance: You have a room full of adults, and you want to play children's games. You want to spend twenty to thirty minutes of meetings doing kindergarten games. This really tweaks my melon. I remember one of John Wayne's sayings: "Let's get on with the rat killing". It is like you are questioning my mental capacity and that does not sit well with me. I guess the question is: at what point in our human lives do we start to regress back to our childhood? Just because we teach children, do we ourselves have to revert back to our childhoods and play those games? And yes, if you are curious, even high school students are still children. What are college students typically, high school kids, unless they are non-traditional, then that is a whole other animal.

Doesn't the Bible, if you believe in that, mention a time to put childish things aside? When do we put childish things aside? Who is the decider who wants to bring the back? Maybe these deciders are the ones who feel better by regressing to childish themes? Maybe these are the ones who cannot seem to grow up? Sometimes I wonder how these supposed leaders got their positions in the first place. It must have been their friends who pushed them ahead to their leadership positions. It doesn't surprise me, in the least.

Which One are You

I tell my students all the time. Which person do you want to be? There is a song by Bob Dylan, Not Dark Yet. He say's "it's not dark yet but it's getting there". It talks about a lot of things he has seen and done and places he has been throughout his life. Every songwriter has a reason for the songs they write. I don't begin to speculate about his reasoning. I have reasons I write books, and it isn't for praise or money, but I have my reasons.

All of us have a beginning, middle, and at some point, will have an ending to our lives. Some will be a smooth transition and others not so smooth. We can all hope for a smooth ending and some of ours just won't turn out that way. We can only hope for the best.

Near the end many of us will have moments of contemplation and resolve. Some of us will see past visions, a flashing before our eyes and others may just go from light to dark in an instance.

I have always heard that it isn't who you will miss when you are gone, it is who is going to miss you, when you are gone. That does seem to make sense.

I tell my students there are two people on this planet. The first person is the one who always tries to do right. Then when bad things happen to them, they say "I always tried to do right, why me"? The second person, who always bypassed the right path. When bad things happen, they say "It was about time. I knew it was coming".

Which one are you? Which one do you strive to be? Which would you rather have engraved on your headstone?

EPILOGUE

I have been adding topics as I go along. Once I address a topic I never go back and edit that topic. That was my feeling and thoughts at the time. Some of these topics may abound again as something popped into my head and made me address them with some other twist. Some topics spill over into other topics, and I think that is just the human reality. Some things are just not cut and dried and simple black and white. Sometimes we have gray areas.

Like I have said before, I am not seeking followers, I am not seeking praise, I am not seeking a key to some hidden pathway to the other side of the moon. I just think that some people think too much. You might be happy to find there is someone else like you on this planet. I do think too much but I do think there are many things that just don't make any sense! In this writing I have detained, retained, maintained, and or entertained a few…

ABOUT THE AUTHOR

I was born in an Appalachian County in central Kentucky. I was once a freshman, At-risk, First-time, Under-prepared college student.

I later received an AS, BS, and MS and was a student worker for my AS and a teaching assistant for my BS and MS degrees. I currently hold 2 undergraduate degrees and 4 graduate degrees and have taken many courses throughout the years.

All of those previous graduate courses are directly related to students and their learning. As I mentioned, my doctorate is in Education not Research. There is a difference, I believe, in both avenues of doctoral programs, but that is another discussion and has been and will be a confusing topic, somewhat possibly a tree branch related to the success of post-secondary college students. I believe successfully taking courses and training directly relating to students and their outcomes has a bearing on how educators relate and come across to students. I believe this to be true. I can't believe anyone in the educational realm is not giving contrary thought to this.

Years later, I am involved in post-secondary education, bringing my ideas, concepts, philosophies, and experiences to my students. Students are the sole reason I do what I do. I will repeat once again: If one single student benefits, I have done my job and fulfilled the purpose of the writing.

NOTES

The End

www.ingramcontent.com/pod-product-compliance
Lightning Source LLC
Chambersburg PA
CBHW050132280326
41933CB00010B/1350